Carissa Licciardello is a director based on Gadigal Land. She was Resident Director at Belvoir St Theatre from 2022 to 2024, following her position as Associate Artist in 2021 and the company's inaugural Andrew Cameron Fellow in 2018 and 2019. Recent work as Director includes—for Belvoir, *Scenes from the Climate Era* (2023); as Director/Adaptor, *Opening Night* (2022) and *A Room of One's Own* (2020/2021); as Associate Director, *Fangirls* (2019/2021), *Counting & Cracking* (2019); as Production Dramaturg, *Nayika: A Dancing Girl* (2024), *Miss Peony* (2023). Other work as Director includes—for Malthouse, *Anna K* (2022); for National Institute of Dramatic Arts, *Machina*l (2022). Carissa is a graduate of the National Institute of Dramatic Arts' Directing course, and was a recipient of NIDA's Glorias Fellowship in 2020.

ELSIE YAGER is a director and writer working between London and Australia. She is a graduate of University of London's MA Theatre Directing course where she studied under Katie Mitchell and received the inaugural Alison Hodge Prize for Excellence in Theatre Directing. Elsie was a JMK Award finalist in 2022, and winner of the Projekt Europa Elevate award. She has a background in devised physical theatre and arts and disability facilitation. Elsie is also a graduate of Actors Centre Australia. Recent work as Director/ Adaptor includes *IPHIGENIA; or the sacrifices of a young woman in nine movements* (2023) and *Colonus* (2022).

BASED ON THE
NOVEL BY
VIRGINA WOOLF

ADAPTED BY
CARISSA LICCIARDELLO
& **ELSIE YAGER**

ORLANDO

CURRENT THEATRE SERIES

First published in 2025
by Currency Press Pty Ltd,
Gadigal Land, Suite 310, 46–56 Kippax Street, Surry Hills, NSW 2010, Australia
enquiries@currency.com.au
www.currency.com.au

in association with Belvoir

Typeset by Brighton Gray for Currency Press.
Printed by Fineline Print + Copy Services, Revesby.
Cover image shows Shannen Alyce Quan, Janet Anderson and Nyx Calder; photo by Daniel Boud. Cover design by Alphabet Studios.

Currency Press acknowledges the Traditional Owners of the Country on which we live and work. We pay our respects to all Aboriginal and Torres Strait Islander Elders, past and present.

A catalogue record for this book is available from the National Library of Australia

Contents

Carissa Licciardello in rehearsal (Photo: Brett Boardman)

Elsie Yager in rehearsal (Photo: Brett Boardman)

Adaptors' note

When we first read *Orlando*, we knew just the barest outline of the story—that a charismatic nobleman travels through time to become a woman. As soon as we picked up the novel, however, we discovered (to our delight) that Woolf had written something far more complex and interesting. Orlando moves from Lord to Lady—and then somehow both and neither—continuing to transform, changeable as the seasons in a journey of endless reinvention.

But it is not only Orlando who transforms—the entire world around them shifts too, over and over again. It became clear to us that *Orlando* is a work about revolution—both the inner revolutions of the individual, and the outer revolutions of history. In Woolf's novel, gender is fluid, but so too is everything else we have been told is fixed: who is in power; what we believe in and why; how we behave and why. Over and over again, what is fixed is proven to be fluid. At its core, this is what we wanted to express onstage in our adaptation.

Our approach to adapting *Orlando* has been through perhaps as many iterations as Orlando themselves, and could have taken many forms. Virginia's novel is an extravagant act of imagination that traverses both time and gender. What an absolute treat—and near-impossible challenge—for two theatre-makers.

We wanted to find a way to translate to the stage what is genuinely magical and ambitious in the novel, and it quickly became clear that we needed to find a new language—one that, although fuelled by Woolf, lives and breathes in the theatre. This meant not relying on Woolf's (fabulous, fabulous) text as narration, but finding a new form that could take an audience inside Orlando's experience. Like Virginia, we looked to history not for an exact representation of the past, but as fuel for a kind of historical expressionism in order to express a truth about Orlando themselves and their relationship to power, gender and selfhood. In doing this, while we have tried to capture the spirit of Virginia's novel, we have also taken a cue from her playful treatment of history and literature, drawing what she pleases from the world to create something new. We have done the same, freely adapting not just Woolf's language but our own forays into the worlds of history, literature, poetry, theatrical tradition, gender, politics, philosophy—and the contemporary world as it has travelled these one hundred years since her writing.

We distilled the work into four distinct worlds—four ages of history, through which four Orlandos travel. Each age has its own customs, its own weather, its own ways of looking and thinking about itself. Each in turn has their own distinct theatrical world in order to express the spirit of each age.

Orlando begins as a nobleman, privy to all the privileges and penalties of being a man in the world, at the height of the Elizabethan era—here, a world of ice where the privileged glide on the frozen River Thames until Elizabeth dies and the fire of revolution thaws this fixed world. Orlando then finds herself a Lady in the Restoration at an endless Ball, introduced, for the first time, to the strict rules accorded to each gender (and the many limitations placed on women). Orlando shifts again into a new self, neither Lord nor Lady, in the Victorian era. Here is a world of fog, and a people possessed by marriage, law and science—by the institution. It is a fearful world, whose citizens in turn cling to what small certainties they have, dividing everything into categories and strictly enforcing them. Finally, Orlando arrives in modernity, where endless trips on the Tube launch us through the speed, variety, possibility of modern life—and the possibilities but also the pressures of self-determination.

Orlando began as a love letter, a beautiful offering from Virginia in honour of Vita Sackville-West. Our adaptation, too, is a kind of love letter—to the various queer communities whose borders we move through and an open invitation to anyone who feels the need to reinvent themselves against the friction of the spirit of the age. Our adaptation is an ensemble piece—where worlds are created and dissolved together, roles taken up and passed off, and Orlando is free to transcend the individual body to become an idea, available for anyone who needs it to take up. It is an offering to a world in dire need of queer laughter and queer joy. It is no frivolous thing to actively find space for joy and imagination in a world that seeks to deny that possibility. Just as struggle is necessary for resistance, so too is staking a claim to the future and imagining together what might be on the other side.

Hopefully you find our adaptation, like Virginia's novel, full of wild fantasy, laughter, and at its heart, a wilful determination—whatever the spirit of the age—to find our way through.

Carissa Licciardello and Elsie Yager

Elsie Yager and Carissa Licciardello in rehearsal (Photo: Brett Boardman)

Shannen Alyce Quan and Emily Havea in rehearsal (Photo: Brett Boardman)

Janet Anderson and Zarif in rehearsal (Photo: Brett Boardman)

Orlando was first produced by Belvoir St Theatre, Gadigal Country, on 30 August 2025, with the following cast and creatives:

ORLANDO 2 & OTHERS	Janet Anderson
NICK GREENE & OTHERS	Nyx Calder
SASHA /NELL/SHELMERDINE	Emily Havea
QUEEN & OTHERS	Amber McMahon
ORLANDO 4 & OTHERS	Nic Prior
ORLANDO 1 & OTHERS	Shannen Alyce Quan
ORLANDO 3 & OTHERS	Zarif

Director & Co-Adaptor, Carissa Licciardello
Co-Adaptor, Elsie Yager
Set Designer, David Fleischer
Lighting Designer, Nick Schlieper
Costume Designer, Ella Butler
Associate Costume Designer, Hailley Hunt
Composer, Alan John
Sound Designer, Kelly Ryall
Associate Sound Designer, Sam Cheng
Choreographer, Shannon Burns
Vocal Coach, Laura Farrell
Roller Skating Coach, P. Tucker Worley
APT Dramaturgy Associate, Brooke Lee
Stage Manager, Luke McGettigan
Assistant Stage Manager, Estelle Gomersall

Nic Prior in rehearsal (Photo: Brett Boardman)

Nyx Calder and Shannen Alyce Quan in rehearsal (Photo: Brett Boardman)

CHARACTERS

ORLANDO

NICK GREENE
QUEEN
SASHA
JESTER
COURTIERS

LADY A/NELL
LADY B
LADY C
LORD A
LORD B
LORD C

WEEPING BRIDE
SUPERSTITIOUS BRIDE
MAD BRIDE
CLERK
REFORMER
SHELMERDINE

YOUTH
BUSINESSWOMAN
BARRISTERS
WOMAN
LESBIAN COUPLE
YOUNG PEOPLE
POLICE OFFICER
YOUNG ADULTS
GYM-GOERS
SCHOOLKIDS
SCHOOLBOY
OLDER WOMAN
STUDENTS
SERVICE WORKERS
TOUR GUIDE
PROTESTORS
SCIENTIST

NOTES

ORLANDO is to be played by four actors.

In the original production, SASHA, LADY A/NELL, and SHELMERDINE were played by the same actor. NICK GREENE and LORD A were also played by the same actor. All other roles are shared among the ensemble.

This play text went to press before the end of rehearsals and may differ from the play as performed.

ACT ONE

THE MASQUE

Out of the darkness comes SIR NICHOLAS GREENE, *an Elizabethan courtier in furs.*

GREENE: In the beginning
there was only Chaos
and the Dark.
Formless
Shapeless
Disordered and disarrayed.
Man had no place in this void.

But then came God
and with His divine hand
He made the Heavens forthwith
In perfect order and balance
Our cosmos.

Behold:

The stars in their firmament, the outermost sphere
Each fixed in their place in the heavenly canopy
Guiding our earthly movements

Suddenly, another COURTIER *skates on, dressed for the Masque: a firmament of stars. They circle an expanse of ice—*

Then, the heavenly bodies—

Another COURTIER *glides on, dressed as the planets—*

Heavy Saturn, planet of limits and penalties
And Jupiter, round of belly, arbiter of Justice,

Mars, the soldier, jealous in honour, quick to quarrel
And radiant Venus, star of love.

Another COURTIER, *as Sun and Moon—*

Then Phaeton, in his chariot, drawing the Sun from East to West,
And Luna, in her silver chair, carrying the Moon.

All orbit each other.

Each resides in their sphere.
Each travel fixed paths
in uniform motion
and perfect balance.
At their centre, lies the Earth,
And its sovereign, Gloriana
Elizabeth herself
Our Queen.

Into the midst of the masque floats QUEEN ELIZABETH—*Gloriana, war queen, at the height of her powers. Her gown is a giant edifice, and she glides without apparent effort.*

As God is to the Heavens, so Gloriana is to Earth
For is she not, of all beings, closest to the Heavens?
See how her face is encircled by rays—
is she not like the Sun, our source of light and power?
See how her face is pale and beauteous—
is she not like the Moon, pure and virginal?

So it turns, this celestial orb,
Each element in divine order,
Each sphere moving in perfect harmony,

As it turns, so does Fortune in its Wheel
The hand of Fate that has brought glory to England
in this, our golden age
Our Queen keeps this universe in orbit
each element in its place
as it has been ordained.

And beyond—nothingness.
The void.
A chaos
to which we shall never return.

May this, the offering of a humble court poet,
do justice to the glory of Elizabeth.
Long may she reign.

He kneels.

COURT: Long live the Queen.

They kneel.

THE CHILD ORLANDO

As they rise—

FIRST COURTIER: Your Majesty
We present to you
The child Orlando.

He is not there.

Orlando …

[*Calling out*] Orlando?

ORLANDO, *late, comes racing into view, and falls to one knee before the* QUEEN.

She holds out her hand. He takes it, and kisses it gently without raising his head.

COURTIER: Your Majesty
The child Orlando.
QUEEN: So this is the young Orlando
Son of William, Earl of Kent?
ORLANDO: Yes, your Majesty.
QUEEN: It is not for a Queen to be kept waiting, Orlando
ORLANDO: Yes, Majesty—forgive me.
In truth—
as I was on my way to meet you
I spied the most glorious oak tree
and became entirely lost in thought.

The COURT *uneasily awaits the* QUEEN*'s response.*

QUEEN: Interesting—

ORLANDO *stays on the ice, head bowed.*

You may raise your head to behold me, child.
ORLANDO: I dare not
Your Majesty.
QUEEN: Is there something you wish to conceal from your Queen? Do your eyes perhaps hold some secret?
ORLANDO: The contents of my heart are an open book to you, Majesty.
But having seen only your hand
I fear that to gaze upon the whole person should dazzle me.
QUEEN: You are sweet, child
But I am curious
If you will not gaze upon your Queen
save for her hand
then what impression will you make of her?
ORLANDO: The hand is eloquent enough, Majesty.
It is a most commanding hand
one that need only raise itself for a head to fall—
a hand that curves
as if made to hold orb and sceptre—
and it is a delicate hand
a nervous hand, perhaps
one that suggests a body strung together by a thousand fears
but that never flinches.
QUEEN: Spoken with the candour of a true innocent!
It is true, child—
I have the body of a weak and feeble woman
but I have the heart and stomach of a King.
Raise your head.

ORLANDO *raises his head.*

Do you find your impression justified?
ORLANDO: Your Majesty is more wondrous than imagination could conceive
Equal parts strength and grace.

The QUEEN *smiles.*

QUEEN: As for my own impression—
Stand, child.

He does.

She circles him.

Violet eyes
A striking head of hair
And a pair of the finest legs a nobleman has ever stood upon.
You are every inch the gentleman
But inwardly … ?

She moves towards him.

Romance—folly—
and youth.
Such youth.
How old *are* you?

ORLANDO: I am not yet seventeen, Majesty.

QUEEN: The very cusp of manhood
but a child still!
May you always remain so—
young of spirit
innocent of heart.

ORLANDO: If your Majesty wishes it, I shall stop Time itself in its endless march.

QUEEN: Ha! You do your duty well, my innocent.

ORLANDO: I desire nothing more than to do my duty to the Crown
as my fathers have done before me
Majesty.

QUEEN: My dear
You are the promise of England.
I see for you a splendid future—
Lands will be granted you, houses assigned you
and titles bequeathed upon you.
You shall know the glory of high achievement
And nothing you desire shall be denied you.

ORLANDO: Majesty
I could not dream of such blessings—

QUEEN: And in return—
you shall be

my Treasurer, my Steward
and as my son.

ORLANDO: Majesty
I will tend upon your every wish.

QUEEN: Then you shall be henceforth known as
the Lord Orlando.

The court melts away ...

and ORLANDO *stands, alone.*

ORLANDO: Lord Orlando.

Slowly, he begins to glide around the ice in a circle ...

A LONG LINE OF FATHERS

After some time—as if recalling a lesson he's been taught—

ORLANDO: Lord Orlando—
Son of William, Earl of Kent;
Son of Nicholas, Baron Hollsworthy;
Son of Richard, a marquess (and famously a drunkard)
Son of Henry, a duke (and secretly a drunkard)
Son of Andrew …
Sir Andrew …

Who built the ancestral home with its three hundred and sixty-five rooms!
Sir Andrew who built the ancestral home with three hundred and sixty-five rooms …

Then Sir Boris, who fought and killed the Spaniard
Sir Herbert, who fought and killed the Frank
Sir Walter, the Egyptian
Sir Randolph, the Turk
And Sir Norbert, the Pole.

And before that—
the first of our name
who … came out of the northern mists wearing coronets on their heads, I suppose

And of this great and illustrious line, comes
Orlando

Orlando …

Who …
rides through battlefields astride a great horse
and strikes many heads off many shoulders.

Orlando …

Who stands on the deck of a tumbling ship
and commands Her Majesty's fleet.

Orlando …
who is friend to bird and beast
who weeps at the sight of the moon
who loves to look to the endless sky
and feel himself forever and ever alone
Orlando the dreamer …
Orlando the poet.

He skates on, lost in thought ...

SASHA

Out of nowhere, a figure darts through the stage like a comet—in breeches and furs, and entirely otherworldly.

ORLANDO *stops in his tracks.*

The stranger stops. They are face-to-face.

ORLANDO *stares. They look calmly back. He bows.*

ORLANDO: Sir.
Or—madam?
SASHA: Your Highness
If one wishes to be formal.
ORLANDO: I beg your pardon?
SASHA: You could also refer to me as Princess Marousha Stanilovska Dagmar Natasha Iliana Romanovitch.
But I prefer
Sasha.

ORLANDO: You are a princess?
But—where is your court? Your attendants? Your King?
SASHA: I prefer to travel alone.

ORLANDO is dumbstruck.

And you are?
ORLANDO: Orlando. Lord Orlando.
SASHA: *Enchanté.*

She takes ORLANDO's hand and kisses it.

Perhaps you can tell me—my Lord—
why it is that your court has taken up residence on this river.
Does it not fear the ice shall crack?
ORLANDO: The river is frozen to a depth of twenty feet or more
and has been for as long as I can remember.
It can hold a court and a carnival and probably a palace besides.
SASHA: I see.
And why does the court conduct itself with such extravagance?
Does the Queen not know the common people starve in the snow?
ORLANDO: Common people?
SASHA: I take it you have yet to meet any, yourself.
ORLANDO: I have not ventured beyond the edge of my estate
beyond the Court.
SASHA: Strange.

She steps towards him.

There is a porpoise in the ice
just below our feet.
ORLANDO: There is?
SASHA: Look.

They look down.

And there—a shoal of eels lying motionless as if in a trance.
There is a whole world beneath your feet, my Lord. And beyond.

She skates away, leaving ORLANDO, struck.

He looks down, gets on his hands and knees, and presses his ear to the ice.

He listens ...

THE JESTER

The QUEEN, *with* ORLANDO *at her feet, watches the Court.*

Three COURTIERS *are presenting a song in honour of the* QUEEN. *They bow, and all applaud.*

And then a COURT JESTER *in skates wobbles onto the ice, leaning on a staff.*

He struggles to move in his skates—tries to slide smoothly, but can't—much to his mock-horror and the mirth of those watching.

He clutches at his belly—hungry. He sweeps off his cap, holds it in his hands like a beggar. He staggers to the court with his hands extended, as if asking for food or gold. They shake their heads at him and laugh, and he staggers about in despair.

He turns and holds his hands out to the QUEEN. *She nods at* ORLANDO, *who hands the* JESTER *a gold coin.*

He takes it greedily—tries to gnaw at it—no good. He throws it away in mock frustration, and rubs his belly.

He looks at the QUEEN *again—and slowly raises his hand to point at her Crown.*

All watch.

She regards him, impassive.

He lowers his finger to point at the QUEEN*'s face and drags his finger across his own neck.*

All hold their breath.

He jams his JESTER*'s hat back on his head, and raises himself as if a King.*

He points to COURTIERS *one by one, slashing his finger across his throat.*

He takes out a match—holds it out like a weapon. Magically, it lights.

He brandishes it—but it is a weak weapon. He extinguishes it.

He holds up his staff—and suddenly it lights—he is holding a wall of flame.

The court titter.

He holds it to the ground as if to melt the ice—then re-considers, and begins to advance on the QUEEN *with the sceptre—*

But then he stops—and as if against his own will, turns the flaming sceptre upside down and puts it in his mouth, swallowing the flames, to the relief of those watching. He stands again, takes his hat off, and gives a deep bow.

JESTER: Your Majesty.

All assembled applaud.

The court melts away, leaving ORLANDO *alone, face-to-face with the* JESTER.

He regards ORLANDO *impassively, then skates away.*

We hear a creaking in the ice—a crack. ORLANDO *looks to it.*

He begins to skate again ...

A NEW LANDSCAPE

And there is SASHA *again, skating opposite him. They circle each other.*

SASHA: I have seen your Tower of London
and the menagerie at its gates
Wild beasts kept under the lock and key of the Queen
Have the elephants committed some treason? Or the lions some crime?
Why else are they contained with muzzle and chain?
ORLANDO: For Her Majesty's entertainment, I suppose.
SASHA: And the gate at the city's entrance
adorned with the heads of your enemies on pikes
Do you regularly rotate these heads or does one simply wait for them to rot away?
ORLANDO: I've never thought to ask.
SASHA: A strange and savage place, this England.
And you, my Lord?
Have you ventured yet beyond the bounds of the court?

ORLANDO: I have seen a whole herd of swine
frozen on the road
immovable!
I've seen fields full of shepherds, ploughmen, and little bird-scaring boys struck stark—as if by magic—in the middle of life!
One with his hand to his nose
Another with a bottle to his lips
A third with a stone raised to throw at the ravens who sat as if stuffed on the hedge within a yard of him!
You were right
There is a whole world beyond this court.
Is this how you spend your days? Every day a new adventure, a fresh sight?

SASHA: Surely you tire of the same vista
Does your heart never long for a new horizon?

ORLANDO: But what of your duties to your Crown? Your family?

SASHA: When my duty outweighs my passions
Then it shall be my north star.
But until then
there is the world
in all its variety
waiting to be discovered.

ORLANDO: You are most extraordinary, Sasha.
I wonder if you would permit me—
it would give me the greatest pleasure in the world to tend upon your every wish
to prove myself worthy of your affections
and win the honour of your love.

SASHA: You imitate a courtier well, my Lord,
but you would do better to speak in your own voice.

ORLANDO: My own … ?

SASHA: What does your heart say?

ORLANDO: You are …

Like an emerald
Like
waves seen from a height
Like the sun on a green hill which is yet clouded—

You are like—an olive tree
A pineapple!
A—

I need another language.
SASHA: You need another landscape.

She skates away ...

A LOVE POEM

ORLANDO *is alone on the ice.*

ORLANDO: *What is your substance whereof are you made,*
That millions of strange shadows on you tend?
Since every one hath, every one, one shade,
And you, but one, can every shadow lend.
Describe Adonis, and the counterfeit
Is poorly imitated after you;
On Helen's cheek all art of beauty set,
And you in Grecian tires are painted new.
Speak of the spring and foison of the year:
The one doth shadow of your beauty show,
The other as your bounty doth appear;
And you in every blessèd shape we know.
In all external grace you have some part,
But you like none, none you, for constant heart.

The entire court has formed around him as he speaks—and he realises with a start that he is staring into the eyes of the QUEEN.

Your Majesty.

He bows.

QUEEN: A most original portrait
And who is the artist, child?
ORLANDO: A poet I have just discovered
A Mr Shakespeare, Majesty.
QUEEN: Ah
A promising young man
And a favourite of mine

He brings honour to our country and this age
as do you, my child.

He bows again.

And to whom do you dedicate this poem?

ORLANDO: To yourself, Majesty
of course.

QUEEN: Then it is not for some sweet young thing who might have your heart?
Some brazen hussy who might tempt you away from my side?
Corrupt my innocent?

ORLANDO: Majesty
My duty is to you
Alone.

The QUEEN *looks long and hard at* ORLANDO. *Then sighs.*

QUEEN: My sweet, dutiful son.
My innocent.

He bows again.

Come.

The court glides away—

save for GREENE.

GREENE: I don't believe we've had the pleasure—
Sir Nicholas Greene.
Court Poet.

ORLANDO: Orlando—
Lord Orlando.

GREENE: Yes
the Queen's favoured courtier.
You make an interesting contribution to our festivities, my Lord
to present the work of a local poet.
It is a shame, however,
that the art of poetry in this country is dead.

ORLANDO: Dead?

GREENE: Yes, and buried, my Lord
Poetry reached its peak
long ago.

All that is worth saying has been said—
and said rather better—
by the Greeks—
the classical poets.
It is upon their foundation that our golden age is built.
Of course, Her Majesty may be partial to these fashionable young writers,
but next to the greats
our new poets are inferior in every respect.

ORLANDO: Sir—
I fail to see how this age can be so inferior …
It has granted us such riches—
Shakespeare has a sonnet for every aspect of love
and his plays are most fantastical
Then there's the work of Mr Spenser, Mr Marlowe—

GREENE: It's precisely these young upstarts we have to thank
for poetry's decline.
These writers are concerned only with feeling—
their personal experience of the world.
Ours is an age marked by the excessive, the indulgent and the self-involved.
Take your dear Shakespeare, for example—
if he can't find the right word, he simply invents one
And this is supposed to be mastery of the English language?
As for Marlowe—
the last I saw of him, he was standing atop a tavern table, rather drunk, which he easily became, and hiccuping out to all assembled
'By my oath, Will!'—
this was to Shakespeare—
'There's a great wave coming and you're on top of it!'
He seemed to be suggesting that we were trembling on the verge of some great revolution in English literature and that Shakespeare was to be a poet of some importance!
Happily for him, he was killed two nights later in a drunken brawl and so did not live to see how his prediction turned out.
No
it pains me to say it,

but I can see no good in the present age and have no hope for the future.

ORLANDO: This is a rather dispiriting assessment.

GREENE: We must simply make the best of it, my Lord
Cherish the past
and honour those writers—
there are still a few of them—
who take antiquity for their model.

ORLANDO: So there are no new landscapes for a poet to explore …

GREENE: It would be the height of self-indulgence to write,
when we already have Sophocles and Homer.
They have mapped every terrain,
scaled every peak of human achievement.
One would be better served to lie in bed of a morning
rolling Cicero along the tongue.

ORLANDO: But … does this satisfy your poet's heart?

GREENE: I'm sorry?

ORLANDO: It seems to me that although a poet may well look to the past
and learn a great deal from it …
Poetry should be a questioning thing—
in love with the world—
Always exploring new territories.
Surely it should not be reduced to mere imitation
It is as Marlowe says—

Nature doth teach us all to have aspiring minds.
Our souls, whose faculties can comprehend
The wondrous architecture of the world,
Still climbing after knowledge infinite,
And always moving as the restless spheres—

... shall *never rest.*

GREENE: A word of warning, my friend.
Look above you
Every planet has its place,
every star its path
It moves as a whole in perfect harmony.

As he speaks, SASHA *glides on in a circle, unaware of* ORLANDO *or* GREENE. ORLANDO *finds his eye drawn to her—*

Should one element move out of place
the whole world might tip on its axis.
Should one break from their assigned path—
Should one venture beyond what is known—
They may be sent spinning into the Dark
Utterly lost.

GREENE *glides away ...*

NEW HORIZONS

... and ORLANDO *skates with* SASHA.

They kiss—and melt into the snow. They sit quietly for a time.

ORLANDO: I know—
you are like—
a fox in the snow.
Like a fox I had as a boy—
a creature with the softest fur, but the sharpest teeth
for it would bite me when I got too near.

SASHA: I should never bite you, my love.

ORLANDO: I know. But you are as fierce as that fox. And stubborn. And beautiful.

SASHA: And you, my little poet—
you are like a million-candled Christmas tree, such as we have in Russia
You are lit from within.

She strokes his face, and they sit, quiet for a while.

ORLANDO: What new sights shall we see tomorrow, my love?

SASHA: The winds are turning
A warm breeze is blowing in from the south—
what do you think, my love?
Is it time, perhaps, for a new horizon?

ORLANDO: You mean—beyond the court? Beyond England?

SASHA: Why not?

ORLANDO: But—you cannot wish to leave me? I am only just beginning to know you.

SASHA: Perhaps
my love
you wish to come with me?
ORLANDO: Go with you?
But—where will we go?
SASHA: Wherever our hearts desire.
Across fields where there is only sky,
And mountains so high we wake among eagles.
ORLANDO: Sasha—*you* are my heart's desire. I wish to be wherever you are.
SASHA: Well, then.
ORLANDO: But—my duty is here. To the Queen. The Crown.
I cannot go.
SASHA: And what about your poet's heart? Do you not have a duty to that?
Do you not long for life—a lover—adventure?
ORLANDO: I *have* a life—and a lover—and every day with you is an adventure, Sasha—I have everything my heart desires.
SASHA: You never wish to venture beyond this court?
ORLANDO: I suppose I could ask to be made Ambassador for a time
Take a station in some far-off kingdom for a while so that you and I may see something of the world together—
SASHA: We are not royal lapdogs
I cannot be commanded *sit* and *stay*
I go where I wish.
ORLANDO: Sasha—I am Treasurer and Steward to the Queen
I can no more cast off my titles than I can my own name,
my very self.
SASHA: Then—
it is settled.
ORLANDO: Just like that?
SASHA: What else can we do? Your path leads you one way, and mine another.
ORLANDO: But—this cannot be!
Whom have I loved, what have I loved, till now?
All my other loves are sawdust and cinders compared to you!
We were brought together by the fates—we are *destined*!

SASHA: I make my own destiny. I am not bound by your fates.
ORLANDO: What if—
what if you were to stay?
SASHA: Stay? For how long?
ORLANDO: Just—just for a little while longer.
SASHA: You wish to cage me, like one of your animals.
ORLANDO: No! Sasha—just think—
If you were to stay, every day could be like this one
Every day some new sight
And every night in each other's embrace—
just as it is now.
SASHA: I do not wish to live each day the same—
I am not made to stay in one place.
And neither, my love, are you.
We are made for adventure.
ORLANDO: Isn't love adventure enough?

She strokes his face.

SASHA: *However well you may feed the wolf*
She will always look to the forest.
ORLANDO: What?
SASHA: Goodbye, Orlando. I shall never forget your tender heart
or your curious mind

—or your fine legs.

She kisses his hand.

ORLANDO: Sasha—please.
It is in my blood
In my birth
And in my stars
It is my destiny.

SASHA *turns.*

SASHA: *Men at some time* must be *masters of their fates:*
The fault, dear Orlando, *is not in our stars,*
But in ourselves.

She skates away.

THE FRAIL AND FEARFUL QUEEN

QUEEN: Here is my innocent.

The QUEEN, *alone. She is much smaller than she was before—wizened, and old.*

She points to the sky.

Tell me.
ORLANDO: That is Orion
With his club and shield
QUEEN: And there?
ORLANDO: Cassiopeia
a Queen on her Throne
QUEEN: And there?
ORLANDO: Regulus
Star of good fortune
Of victory

The QUEEN *strokes his cheek.*

QUEEN: This is my victory.
Come
Help me.

He goes to her. She takes his arm, and begins to hobble, ever so slowly, around the ice.

You are the limb of my infirmity
The oak tree on which I lean.
The son of my old age.
ORLANDO: You have not aged a day, my Queen.
Your youth is without end.
QUEEN: How you have grown into the ways of the court. You flatter with such ease.
ORLANDO: It is the truth, Majesty.
QUEEN: No, my child
I am grown old and worn and bent before my time
As the crimson velvet turns to dust

The ring loses its ruby
And the eye which was once so lustrous shines no more.
ORLANDO: Not for you, Majesty—
Your everlasting rule has been ordained by God
QUEEN: Yet I am flesh and blood, like you.
We that sing and dance above must one day lie below.
It is a truth of the world, my innocent—
All ends in death.
ORLANDO: Majesty—
Why do you speak of this?
QUEEN: I am grown weary, Orlando.
I see always the glistening poison drop, and the long stiletto
Hear always the whisper, the curse
One hand holds the sceptre and the other clutches a mirror for fear of
spies always behind me
To be a Queen is to be strung together by a thousand fears
And live ever in wait of death.
I do not have the strength to wait much longer.
ORLANDO: Live on for my sake, then, Majesty
For I cannot fathom who I would be without you.
What is a nobleman without a Queen?
QUEEN: Perhaps
you would be free to become another self entirely
As I would have been
Had I not worn the Crown.
ORLANDO: The Queen herself may be mortal
But England—
your Empire—
is forever.
QUEEN: Even an Empire can turn to dust.
ORLANDO: Then we skate on nothing thicker than a knife's blade.
QUEEN: That's it, my innocent.
You are beginning to lose your illusions
as one must
if they wish to grow up.

She shuffles away, of her own accord. ORLANDO *watches her go.*

The ice creaks.

The court glide on.

FIRST COURTIER: Her Majesty
Queen of England
has died.

The ice cracks.

FIRST COURTIER: Long live the King.
COURT: Long live the King.

ORLANDO *looks at his noble garments.*

And slowly peels them off.

He holds his furs before him, shivering in the cold—

and another ORLANDO, *wearing a dress, steps onto the ice.*

The two ORLANDO*s stand, staring at each other in shock.*

And suddenly, there is the JESTER *from before.*

JESTER: The new King is dead.
The whole world is upside down—
Now anything is possible.
Long live the Revolution!

He lights the fire of revolution—Elizabeth's world dissolves.

And suddenly, a suspended moment—our two ORLANDO*s, alone.*

They regard each other.

FIRST ORLANDO: Orlando?
I see …

Then, as if some silent understanding has passed between them, the first ORLANDO *steps away into the darkness—and our second* ORLANDO *is alone.*

She stands—and takes in her gown—takes in herself—

ORLANDO: I must say this is much improved.

And all of a sudden—

ACT TWO

A NEW WORLD: SOCIETY

—and suddenly, a Restoration ball. Three LADIES *and three* LORDS, *frocked and wigged—they are dancing silhouettes; metred, ordered, precise.*

LADY A: I say,
fine weather we're having
LORD A: Indeed
I haven't seen a storm cloud in nary a year

The couples part, and reform—

LADY B: And what fine ribbons you have, sir
LORD B: My thanks, good Lady
I procured these in Toulouse
One can always look to the French for the latest fashions
LADY B: Indeed.

The couples part, and reform—

LADY C: And how is the health of your wife,
my Lord?
LORD C: Much improved, I thank you
Certainly one of the great dangers to women in this age
is the rolling of an ankle in a *quadrille*
LADY C: Indeed.

Ding ding ding—a GENTLEMAN *raises a glass. The music ceases.*

LORD A: A toast:
Now with general peace our world is blest
Where once our state was riven by unrest.
Men tried, in flames, to wrap a nation's fate
While chaos reigned, our peace we did await.
But fire's hungry Passion were stamped out
And reign of Reason, 'twere then brought about

No more dark clouds draw down the labouring sky,
Only fair winds for sailing by.
And now the sun, round which the planets fly
beams brightly down on all go dancing by.
And now, the most esteemed of our great state
Do flock to London to augment their fate.
All those who do possess gentility
Form the heart of London Society.
The Restoration of King and Crown,
brings endless summer to Olde London town.

All applaud.

The GENTLEMAN *spies* ORLANDO.

Ah!
And this evening, ladies and gentlemen,
making her maiden voyage into Society,
we have a debutante!

All turn to look at ORLANDO.

Tell us—
who are you?

ORLANDO *looks about her—all eyes are fixed on her.*

ORLANDO: I am Orlando.
LORD A: Presenting
to the Lords and Ladies of Society
the Lady Orlando!

All bow and curtsey to the LADY ORLANDO.

A NEW DESTINY

Immediately—a GENTLEMAN *swoops in to take* ORLANDO*'s hand.*

A partnered dance, in neat lines.

LORD C: Lady Orlando.

He guides her through the dance.

What a fine complexion you have
and to what advantagc it looks against your silks.

You shall have a fine time in Society—
Doubtless you will pick up some noble Prince and reign,
his consort, over half of Yorkshire.

ORLANDO: Oh my—

The dance sweeps them apart—and another GENTLEMAN *steps in.*

LORD B: Lady Orlando
How fashionable you are
and how this gown becomes you.
True it is that the most glamorous of persons flock to London
Certainly you shall be famous throughout the city
for your taste and refinement.

ORLANDO: Thank you, sir—

The dance sweeps them apart—and another GENTLEMAN *steps in.*

LORD A: Lady Orlando
You dance with the agility of a sprite.

ORLANDO: And you, sir, with the—poise of a peacock.

LORD A *laughs like a tinkling bell.*

LORD A: My Lady, what sparkling wit!
How clever you are
Perhaps I shall elicit your criticisms on the contents of my poems.

ORLANDO: Poems? You are a poet?

LORD A: I am known to jot a little doublet now and again
to exercise my wit
but many in Society are pleased to be witty.

The dance shifts, and now it is the women who pass each other—

LADY C: Lady Orlando
What an entrance you have made.
Launched on the sparkling waters of Society
and with some splash and foam at that.

ORLANDO: I am most flattered by these attentions—
although they are somewhat strange, considering
no-one knows a thing about me.

LADY C: The fact that you are here at all tells us all we need to know.
To gain entry to Society is the aim of every well-bred person

Every man, it is said, has been a Prime Minister,
and every woman mistress of a King.
Certain it is that all are brilliant, and all famous.

ORLANDO: Famous?

LADY C: Indeed.
Every man and woman here is destined
for greatness.

ORLANDO: Of what kind?

LADY C: Whatever their heart desires.

ORLANDO: And you have no higher duty?

LADY C: What higher duty is there?
We dance
Drink
Dress in finery
Pursue, that is to say, *life*—
and a lover.
The perfect occupation for a young woman in her prime.

*The women sweep away into the dance—*ORLANDO *is momentarily still, alone—*

ORLANDO: Life—
and a lover …

The dancers circle ORLANDO, *a parade of potential lovers, until ...*

MAN MAY LOOK THE WORLD FULL IN THE FACE …

LADY B *steps into the centre of the room.* ORLANDO *is mesmerised. She holds her handkerchief before her, and elegantly lets it flutter it to the ground.* ORLANDO *stoops to catch it.*

ORLANDO: Yours
my Lady.

LADY B: Oh—thank you, my dear. You are most gracious.

ORLANDO: Of course, madam. It is a pleasure to assist one so beautiful.

LADY B *holds her handkerchief aloft again and drops it.*

LADY B: [*as if to be heard by the room at large*] Oh! How clumsy of me!

ORLANDO *picks it up again and returns it.*

ORLANDO: No matter, Lady.
What you lack in a firm grasp, you make up for in beauty.
LADY B: Thank you, dear.

She holds her handkerchief aloft again.

ORLANDO: My Lady … do you wish to dispose of your handkerchief altogether?
LADY B: My dear
[*Conspiratorially*] I mean to woo.
ORLANDO: How clumsy of me! I am of course most flattered.
And it would be my heart's greatest wish to tend to your every desire.
LADY B: Not *you,* my dear! A gentleman.
ORLANDO: Oh. I see.
LADY B: Can a woman love a woman so?
ORLANDO: It is a woman I loved before
And so, I suppose, I may still love a woman now.
LADY B: How peculiar.
Regardless
in Society, it is not for a woman to pursue
but to be pursued.
ORLANDO: But—if I know what I desire
why should I not speak it plainly?
LADY B: This is too much the manner of the gentleman.
Such an approach is, how does one put it—
too direct.
A Lady must go roundabout.

… *BUT WOMAN MUST TAKE A SIDELONG GLANCE*

—and at once, the LADIES *are gathered together, fans poised,* ORLANDO *with them.*

The GENTLEMEN *stand at a distance, watching.*

LADY A: What fine gentlemen there are to attend us
I hear the Marquis of Salisbury is to join us shortly.

LADY B: Oh, what a gentleman.
He has the largest estate in all of Hampshire.
LADY C: And the Archduke Harry, a fine specimen.
He has the largest Fortune in all of East Anglia
has published four bestselling books
funded three expeditions to the Pacific
And is rumoured for a knighthood.
ORLANDO: And … are we simply to wait for these fine gentlemen to approach?
LADY A: Heavens, no, dear.
LADY C: One need not always speak
in order to speak.
ORLANDO: I do not follow, Lady.
LADY C: There is an entire language
in the movement
of a fan.

The women whip their fans open.

Observe.

The LADIES *begin to cross the dancefloor, flirting with their fans—the* LORDS *are drawn to them, as if on a string—then the* LADIES *flick their fans open in front of their faces—the* LORDS *draw back. There is something of the tango about it—and it continues—the* LADIES *invite—the* LORDS *respond—the* LADIES *hide—the* LORDS *draw back.*

In a moment, the groups separate again, LORDS *and* LADIES. LADY C *smiles at* ORLANDO*—*

ORLANDO: It seems most delicious—to refuse, and see him frown.
LADY C: More delicious still—to yield, and see him smile.
ORLANDO: And now? They approach?
LADY B: Certainly not. The game has only just begun—
and we have only deployed the first weapon in our arsenal.
Regard—

LADY B *sweeps her handkerchief into the air—the men snap around to watch her—delicately, she lets it fall. A* GENTLEMAN *sweeps in to collect it as it flutters to the ground—then* LADY A *lets hers fall, and*

LADY B, *in a cascade of fabrics, and each man sweeps forward to catch a handkerchief and return it to its owner—*

The LADIES *giggle shyly, and take back their handkerchiefs.*

The groups separate again.

ORLANDO: Surely nothing is more heavenly than to resist and to yield, to yield and to resist. It seems to throw the spirit into such a rapture as nothing else can.

LADY A: There is perhaps one thing more satisfying—
when one may deliver a decisive final blow.

LADY A *sweeps into the centre of the room—takes hold of her skirts—and exposes—her ankle.*

The men stop dead—frozen. They begin to go rather red in the face.

LADY A *hides her ankle and releases them—they gasp, breathing again.*

ORLANDO: If the sight of an ankle means death to an honest fellow
then, in all humanity, should we not keep them covered?

LADY B: Ah, but where's the fun in that?
'Tis all part of the dance, Lady Orlando.
One must simply know how to lead it.

The LORDS *and* LADIES *sweep into the dance again—each employ the fan, the handkerchief, the ankle as they please—a tango between resist and yield, resist and yield—*

Finally, ORLANDO *joins in—at the centre of it all, she holds a handkerchief aloft. All freeze to behold it.*

She lets it flutter to the ground—and a GENTLEMAN *steps forward to catch it.*

LORD B: Yours, I believe.

ORLANDO: *Thank* you, sir.
How swiftly you came to my aid.
Such speed—such strength.
I should have been lost without your assistance.

LORD B: The pleasure, Lady
is all mine.

ORLANDO: What a debt of gratitude I owe to you
My rescuer.
Oh
I feel rather faint.

Her knees start to give way—

LORD B: You may rest in my arms, Lady.
ORLANDO: Oh, thank you.
LORD B: How pale and weak you seem
as if you might fade away!
ORLANDO: Yes
with such a delicate constitution
a stray breeze may knock me to the floor.
LORD B: Might I procure you a refreshment
some sustenance to fortify your strength?
A cucumber sandwich?
A tiny slice of beef, perhaps?
ORLANDO: Oh … but I couldn't.
LORD B: Just a little of the fat, Lady?
Let me cut you just the tiniest little slice the size of your fingernail.
ORLANDO: You tempt me sir
but I simply couldn't.
LORD B: Madam
If you think I shall yield to your refusals
you underestimate my stamina
I can go on
and on
Unless of course, you simply mean to inflame my ardour
with sweet
reluctant
amorous delay …
ORLANDO: Well …
I would
if you wished it
just have the very smallest
thinnest
tiniest
sliver in the world.

He shudders in pleasure.

They turn and part, sweeping back into their separate spheres, women here, men there.

LADY B: Well?
ORLANDO: This is surely the chiefest delight in all the world.
Praise God I'm a woman!

The LADIES *laugh.*

The dance spins around ORLANDO *and they move from partner to partner—*

ORLANDO: What a sparkling day!
LORD C: Indeed.
ORLANDO: What voluptuous ribbons!
LORD B: Charmed.
ORLANDO: Such diaphanous silks!
LADY C: What charm!
LORD A: What youth!
LORD B: What legs!

And all at once the dance swirls into—

THE DEBUTANTE'S MISTAKE

Stillness. Society gathered around ORLANDO—LORDS *with hands on hips,* LADIES *fluttering fans.*

LORD C: Lady Orlando,
you have made a swift impression
on our slice of Society.
Where have you been till now
that you have not before
graced us with your presence?
ORLANDO: I was not formerly acquainted in the pleasures
and idle entertainments of Society.
In truth, I have been rather occupied until now
with matters of the heart.
LADY C: What better occupation is there for a Lady?

ORLANDO: But I was always promised a splendid future
So I suppose it is time to turn my mind to my career.

The LADIES *and* LORDS *chuckle generously.*

LADY B: Her career!
The Lady has a sparkling wit.
LORD B: You have a queer humour indeed, Lady.
Might I be so bold,
as to ask from whence your charms and graces hail?
Do I know your father?
A Lady with such violet eyes
Such a fine head of hair
And a pair of the most fabulous legs a woman has ever stood upon
must derive from a most famous family?
ORLANDO: My father was William, Earl of Kent.
And I myself have been Treasurer and Steward to a Queen.

The LORDS *and* LADIES *laugh.*

LADY B: Treasurer and Steward! Oh my …
LORD C: I think our Lady doth mean to mock our questioning
Yet when it falls from such a sweet mouth
and with such humour, even mockery brings mirth.
LADY C: [*referring to* LORD C] Our Lordship wears the Order of the Garter
And is a great beloved of the King.
LORD C: [*with a bow*] I am pleased only to serve.
LADY A: His Lord is too modest.
LORD A: I must ask—as I have not heard of a Lady Orlando
amongst the promising families of London
—from whence do you hail?
ORLANDO: I have an estate outside London,
where I have spent much of my youth.
LADY B: You 'have' an estate—what a curious slip of the tongue, Lady—
You mean to say your father has?
ORLANDO: No—the estate has been promised to me alone.

Some confused chuckles from Society.

LORD B: And besides her—mischievous humour,
What other talents does her Lady possess?
ORLANDO: Talents—
LADY C: A Lady in Society must have one or more accomplishments
Myself, for example, have embroidered my own gown—
For some it is the needle, for others the lute,
Or perhaps your Ladyship has the voice of a nightingale?
ORLANDO: Well—
As a child I trained in fencing, and can ride horseback as well as any nobleman—

The LORDS *and* LADIES *laugh ...*

but above all else
at heart
I am a poet.
LORD A: A poet?
ORLANDO: Aye, sir.

A strange silence.

LORD A: A poetess!
How—
novel.
LADY C: [*referring to* LORD A] His Lordship is—besides his many achievements
in science, law and diplomacy—
one of the foremost poets of our age
His latest collection sold five hundred copies!
LORD A: One must remember poetry is harder to sell than prose
And of course, there is the conspiracy against me—
LADY B: He is a most remarkable poet—in my humble estimation
And the estimation of many well-respected gentleman too.
ORLANDO: Well, then! It is a pleasure to meet another enthusiast.

Deathly silence.

LORD A: Enthusiast?
I am more than an enthusiast.
LADY C: Our Lordship is a poet of some weight—
LORD A: Poetry is no place for the enthusiast
It is rather more stern and serious an undertaking than that.

And I am far from *enthusiastic*
about the deplorable condition of our native tongue
and the vulgarity of poetry in our present time.
Ours is an age marked by the excessive, the indulgent and the self-involved—by those poets who tend toward the Romantic.

The LADIES *show their approval.*

LADY A: How *lucky* we are, my Lord, to be blessed with such intellect!

ORLANDO: I do apologise, my Lord. I did not intend to demean your—talents—

LORD A: [*graciously*] No matter, Lady.
Who does not love to hear a pretty verse or sweetly-sung phrase?
Poetry needs its enthusiasts
But perhaps it is best they leave the writing to the experts.

LORD B: Besides, what a terrible exertion
for one who should lie lapped like a lily in folds of silk,
worshipped by many a lover!
To write, or read, or think—
surely such efforts cloud your beauty
and furrow your brow.

LORD C: You may be grateful, Lady Orlando,
to be spared the burden of such labours
and be free to enjoy the pleasures of life.

The LORDS *spin away from her ...*

THE LADIES IN PRIVATE

The LADIES *dance prettily, observed at some distance by the* LORDS.

ORLANDO: I seem to have fallen afoul of our gentleman companions
yet I haven't the faintest idea how.

LADY B: A gentleman's confidence can be a fragile thing, Lady Orlando.
A wrong word—a stray glance—
a blink in the wrong direction from a Lady admirer—
and it may all come crashing down.

ORLANDO: Lord. How concerning.
Yet that aside, I suppose they are all rather impressive, aren't they?

LADY A: They certainly appear so—

They speak behind their fans as they dance—

But that one slobbers like a hound when he seeks to kiss you—
LADY B: That one's droning fairly puts one to sleep—
LADY C: And that one is the most insufferable bore.
I could give you the entire history of his struggle with
the gout, the plague, the ague.
ORLANDO: Good grief! Then why, for God's sake,
do you lavish them with such extraordinary praise?
LADY A: We do not flatter men
out of respect for their person, or station
We flatter them out of respect for our own.
LADY C: Men may, if they wish, deny us our own estates,
our own fortunes,
even a modest education.
LADY B: And so, one must remember—
If a Lord writes a verse
he is not a great wit, but the greatest poet since Homer.
Should a Lord seek to woo,
he is not a fine lover, but a lover to rival Mark Antony.
When he encounters a rain puddle he is Francis Drake
When he kills a mouse he is William the Conqueror.
LADY C: It is tedious, yes—
but if she wishes to experience the delights of life,
a Lady must stay in man's good graces.

The LADIES *swirl away.*

The LORDS *and* LADIES *gather* ORLANDO *into a dance reminiscent of the opening ...*

THEY ACT THE PARTS OF MEN AND WOMEN WITH GREAT VIGOUR (OR, TIME PASSES)

They dance—

Time passes ... has ORLANDO *been here for hours or months? The dance becomes more laboured, the poised silhouettes melting in exhaustion—*

*Until—*ORLANDO *and* LORD B*—they dance and speak slowly under the weight of exhaustion—*

LORD B: Once
when I was abroad in Sweden
I shot an elk
ORLANDO: How manly
LORD B: Indeed
ORLANDO: And … was it a very big elk
LORD B: Not as big as the reindeer I shot in Norway
ORLANDO: And … have you ever shot a tiger
LORD B: I once shot an albatross
ORLANDO: And … is an albatross as big as an elephant
LORD B: Smaller than an elephant, but twice as fearsome.
ORLANDO: How terribly
terribly
boring.

Oops. They look at each other. With quavering voice—

LORD B: I understand.
I've never been to Sweden.
And I've never shot an elk.
Indeed, I'd much rather sit at home
working at my embroidery.

ORLANDO *stares. The* LORD *suddenly becomes aware of the other dancers.*

Did I say embroidery? I meant to say—
polishing my medals.
Which I won.

In battle.

For bravery.

ORLANDO: No doubt.

The LORD *gives a short bow, and departs.*

Then I shall never be a poet
famed throughout the land
And I shall never be able to challenge a man
or tell him he lies in his teeth,
or draw my sword and
run him through the body!
And I shall never sail in a merchant ship,
or lead an army,
or wear seventy-two different medals on my chest.
True, I never much cared for such things before—
but at least I had the liberty.

Is this the height of my great Destiny?
All this going roundabout never seems to get one anywhere
Perhaps it is time to go straight to the heart of the matter!

... and then, suddenly ...

THE GENTLEMAN'S PRIVATE PARLOUR

The LORDS *are perched around the harpsichord, smoking clay pipes—the atmosphere of a smoking room at three a.m. Far off, in another world, the women move as one, dancing but leaning on each other as if beginning to melt with exhaustion.*

LORD A: *An Ode to the Muse—*

She walks on air, not 'pon the earth,
Her grace proclaims her heavenly birth;
Clouds part, birds sing, eyes brim with tears,
Whene'er my heart's true twin is near
Till Lust is spent and eyes see clear;
Where once the sound of love did trumpet—
Now she's just a common strumpet.

The other LORDS *laugh.*

LORD C: Behold! My verse;

He clears his throat—

There once was a lady called Kitty —
Lady Orlando!

The GENTLEMEN *see* ORLANDO *and snap to attention.*

ORLANDO: Gentlemen
Speak you some poetry?
LORD C: Ah, that—
that is nothing but a parlour game.
A little wordplay between gentleman
Nothing that would be of great interest to a Lady.
ORLANDO: On the contrary, I am, as you know, quite the enthusiast and would love nothing more than to hear a little wordplay.
LORD B: My Lady—
It would not be polite to expose a woman such as yourself to the cut and thrust of male conversation.
ORLANDO: I assure you gentlemen
I am no stranger to the society of men.
Since the earliest days of my youth I have wielded swords with sharper edges than your words.
LORD C: There's that peculiar humour again.
You make a charming attempt at wit, madam, but perhaps it is best you keep to the company of your fellow maidens?
ORLANDO: But sir
you would not be so impolite as to deny a Lady the privilege of your great Genius?
LORD A: … I suppose not.
ORLANDO: Allow me simply to sit at your feet and worship.

The GENTLEMEN *are uncertain.* LORD B *gives a deep bow.*

LORD B: Of course, my Lady!
How pleasant it is to have the company of one so gracious.
After all, women are a poet's great inspiration, are they not?
LORD A: *The bright Orlando's praise rehearse,*
In warbling words, and glittering verse,
that smoothly run into a song,
and gently melt upon the tongue.

ORLANDO: How very pretty your verse is, sir!
And how flattering to be considered a Muse.
Although—
if you will allow me—
it is one thing to be praised in song,
And quite another to sing in one's own voice.
LORD A: *Prepare the hallowed strain my Muse*
Thy softest sounds, and sweetest music choose.
LORD C: Or better yet, say nothing.
ORLANDO: Pardon?
LORD B: Ah, but to put pen to paper, my dear, one must employ thought!
And the act of thinking does flush a Lady's cheek worse than brandy!
If you have any concern for your complexion—
LORD B: One of the chiefest beauties of a Lady!
With glowing eye and damask cheek
By nature obedient, chaste and meek!
ORLANDO: Another pretty phrase, sir.
However—if I may—
I regret to inform you gentlemen that
judging by my own short experience of the sex
women are not, by nature, obedient, chaste or meek at all.
They can only attain these graces by the most tedious discipline—
without which they may enjoy none of the delights of life—!
LORD B: But what delights are yours to enjoy!
Praised by every quill,
Worshipped by ev'ry lip?
ORLANDO: Many words said about her, yes,
But none her own.
LORD C: And all the better for it—
ORLANDO: I beg your pardon?
LORD A: What we mean to say, my Lady—
is that—traditionally—it is not for the muse to speak
but to inspire speech
through the vessel of a true Genius.
ORLANDO: May not a woman be such a vessel?

The GENTLEMEN *titter.*

LORD A: It is not an—ordinary—occupation for a Lady …
Given her proclivities for paduasoy over poetry
It has been rumoured that one or two such women exist in the Catholic nations
yet of course, the Italians are of a different temperament.
They suffer from an overgrowth of Passion
unfortunately coupled with a deficit of Reason
and thus lack the command of rhyme and meter
that keeps the tumults of their emotions in order.
'Tis the same for the poetess.

ORLANDO: I'm sorry?

LORD B: Men and women, by their nature, are suited to different pursuits.

LORD C: Women were formed to temper mankind,
to bring balance, harmony, order.
They should soothe men into tenderness and compassion,
not set an edge upon their minds.

ORLANDO: My. You seem to be experts on the nature of women
as if you yourselves were the Lords of Creation!
But—of course you *are* blessed with great intellect.

LORD A: It is a simple fact, Lady—

Two principles in human nature reign;
Passion, to urge, and Reason, to restrain.

These principles are as opposed to each other as is Night to Day—
or Man to Woman
The one of whom is made for intellect—
the other, for emotion.

LORD B: Just as woman's hand, delicate as it is, serves better to ply the needle—
Man's hand, with its strength and power, is better to wield the pen.

LORD C: Neither is woman suited to the labours of the mind.
The thoughts of woman dwells on trifles and fancies—
A woman has—notions, not thoughts …

ORLANDO: Then pray, allow me to share a notion of mine—
I know many a Lord occupied with such trifles
Who loves to sport a ribbon,
to tend, of a night, to their needlework
and would weep at the thought of a torn piece of lace.

Equally, I know ladies who read Shakespeare
And ride horses and play games of hazard with the best of them!

LORD A: My Lady, we admire your *passionate* speech
but 'tis hard to grasp at your meaning when it is so engulfed by emotion.

ORLANDO: Emotion? But—you are a poet!
Do you not feel things strongly?
Surely you would not say that passion has no place in poetry?

LORD A: A gentleman does not debase himself with the chaos of emotion.
When a man writes of feeling it is not the weeping, womanly kind
He writes of something more …
transcendent.

LORD B: Everything has its place, of course—
And *Passion, the spring of motion, acts the soul—*
But Reason's *comparing balance rules the whole.*

LORD C: Reason must govern Passion
as Man must rule Woman. 'Tis the way of the world.
What if the foot, ordain'd the dust to tread,
Or hand to toil, aspired to be the head?

ORLANDO: And what of the woman who feels she has sufficient command of Reason
and desires to write herself?

LORD B: But, my Lady—it is well known that women have no desires —only affectations.

LORD A: And without desires, well—
unfortunately, her poetry cannot be of the slightest interest
to anyone.

The GENTLEMAN *smile at* ORLANDO.

ORLANDO: Perhaps you are right, gentleman. It is I that am the fool.
Here I thought poets were those who feel more, think more
love more freely than mere mortals
But to hear you all speak of women—your *Muse—*
I am beginning to be convinced you have never met one in your lives!
Your verses may be clever but they bear no resemblance to the real thing.

And you say you are ruled by Reason
All you do is proclaim your virtues, so that women may praise you
Deny her speech, lest a woman laugh at you
You are utterly at the mercy of a Lady's ankle yet go about as if you were God's gift to the green Earth—
Heavens! What fools you are!

The men are silent.

LORD A: My Lady—

His manner has entirely changed.

We have permitted you to join us for a short while
But surely a woman must know very well
that though a man may read her his poems, praise her womanly charms and admire her appearance
this by no means signifies that he respects her opinion
admires her understanding
or will refuse
though the sword is denied him
to run her through the body with his pen.
Women are but children of a larger growth.
A man of sense only humours them.
You would do better, my dear, to think less of poetry
and think more of taffeta.

The men chuckle and melt away, leaving ORLANDO *alone.*

POETRY

ORLANDO *sits at the harpsichord, playing a single note over and over. She begins to slump over the keys as she plays, until her head lands flat on top of the instrument. She is still.*

LADY A: My Lady! Are you ill?

ORLANDO *sits bolt upright.* LADY A *watches in alarm.*

ORLANDO: No!
Thank you, my Lady. I am perfectly well. Just a little weary.

LADY A: Weary! I should have thought a debutante would find her first ball rather intoxicating.

ORLANDO *looks at* LADY A *warily.*

ORLANDO: At first, perhaps, it was
But between all the swooning and sighing
and fussing and flattering
and biting my tongue and gritting my teeth and wishing I had my sword at hand—
I am rather at the end of my tether.

LADY A: Thank God you said so! For I myself have had rather enough of playing the part of Lady for one night.
The truth of the matter is, I'm in desperate need of a fix.

LADY A *looks about her, then pulls a long thin pipe from her bodice, and lights up.*

ORLANDO: Are Ladies permitted to smoke?

LADY A: I like to see what I can get away with on occasion.

ORLANDO: How unexpected. You play the part of the Lady so well.

LADY A: I've had plenty of practice. But one does rather tire of the airs and graces after a time—and then I wish to be, like the gentleman more direct.

ORLANDO: Then—we may speak freely?

LADY A: By all means.

ORLANDO: Praise be to God! I was beginning to lose my senses!
Society is utterly *absurd.*
One may converse at length, only to find nothing of substance has been said. No-one may utter something insightful, or wise, or *real.*
And of course, one has no shortage of pleasures in Society—
the music is fine, the dresses to die for—lovers, I have in plenty, but *Life*
which is, after all, of *some* importance
is nowhere to be found!

LADY A: 'Tis *full of sound and fury, signifying nothing.*

ORLANDO: Exactly!
[*Realising*] You know Shakespeare?

LADY A: I'm acquainted with some of his works.
But I rather prefer his plays to his poetry.

ORLANDO: I can't begrudge you that.

LADY A: 'Tis a delight to hear his words spoken aloud—to hear the audience hush—to watch a man fight to the death—or see a Lady cry.

ORLANDO: But alas—what a pity—that a Lady shall never speak Shakespeare upon the stage.

LADY A: *Au contraire*, my dear.
You will find, of late, that women are sanctioned to take to the London stage.

ORLANDO: You mean—

LADY A: They may play the part of maid and damsel
The ingenue—and even the gentleman who woos her.
In silk stockings no less.

ORLANDO: With her ankles exposed? Do not the gentlemen pass out in the stalls?

LADY A: No doubt on some occasions.
And perhaps even a Lady or two may swoon.
You blush!
An actress may go about in skirts one day
and breeches the next
and thus court gentleman and Lady alike.

ORLANDO: But—surely one finds it confusing, sustaining such different parts.

LADY A: On the contrary—it rather doubles the pleasures of life.

ORLANDO: But—they are in direct opposition
For man is divided as sheerly from woman
as night from day.

LADY A: And what of twilight?
What of the slow creep of dawn? The gentle gradient of dusk?
Besides
surely you have already begun to see
All the world's a stage, and all the men and women ...

ORLANDO: *Merely players.*

LADY A: *And one must*
in their time
play many parts.

A new piece of music begins.

And there's my cue.

NELL GWYNN

LADY A *takes the floor—and begins to sing. The song is slow, unmetered, seductive—*

and bit by bit, the LADY A *begins to transform herself—*

she reveals under her skirts a pair of men's brogues, socks and garters under boxer briefs—

She takes a ribbon from around her ankle and wraps it about her neck like a GENTLEMAN*'s pussy bow—she dons a jacket, sweeps off her wig, puts on a tricorn hat—and is transformed into* NELL GWYNN*—here a kind of Restoration Marlene Dietrich.*

A microphone comes out of nowhere—a spotlight forms—and it is as if we are almost gazing through time into the 1920s—

The other LADIES *are nowhere to be seen—but the* LORDS *become* NELL*'s supporting act—carrying her around on the harpsichord, travelling with candelabras … .*

Until the song winds to a close.

NELL *tips her hat to* ORLANDO*, kisses her on the hand, and departs.*

ORLANDO *is alone—*

until a third ORLANDO *appears, in Victorian garb of mixed gender—a Victorian cycling suit.*

They circle each other—and begin a slow partnered dance, alternating the parts of LORD *and* LADY.

Our second ORLANDO *departs—leaving our third alone, as fog begins to fill the dance floor …*

ACT THREE

A new ORLANDO *in a Victorian cycling suit—alone—in swirling fog.*

ORLANDO: Hello?

Hello?

What a strange landscape.

Where in the world could I be?

A bell tolls, and a solemn procession of black-clad Victorians emerge from the fog in top hats and bonnets, accompanied by funereal music.

PRIEST: [*intoning*] Blessed are The Respectable
who dwell in office and law court,
virgins and city men,
lawyers and doctors,
those who prohibit,
those who deny,
those who do reverence without knowing why.
Blessed are those who bring direction and discipline
to these dark and uncertain times.
And blessed is she who guards Virtue in the home
She who brings Harmony, Balance, Order—
the Angel in every house.

A WEEPING BRIDE *all in black emerges from the fog. She appears to be weeping.*

She glides forward in procession, and as she passes ORLANDO, *she drops a handkerchief. They stoop to pick it up—*

ORLANDO: Madam—your handkerchief.
BRIDE: Oh—thank you.

She takes a shuddering gasp.

ORLANDO: Do you weep, madam?

BRIDE: Yes—
But it is most pleasant to weep
for is it not in woman's nature?
ORLANDO: I would hope not.
But what occasion brings you to weep so?
BRIDE: [*weeping harder*] Only the happiest day of my life
To be joined in holy matrimony to my Thomas
my husband, and my life
and then to bear him a child.
ORLANDO: I see—
BRIDE: And then another
and another
and another
my whole future one long succession of childbirths …
ORLANDO: Madam—

ORLANDO *draws close.*

If you are in need of rescuing from such a fate, just say the word, and I shall—
BRIDE: [*drawing back in horror*] No!
My wedding band will be one with my finger
And I shall never, never take it off!
Not the Archbishop nor the Pope nor Queen Victoria on her throne could force me to do that.
My Thomas shall put it on my finger; and I shall sleep in it
work in it
be buried in it,
and by its gleam shall I be assigned my station among the Angels!

A black wedding veil is lowered over her face. She processes on and away.

ORLANDO: What an unfortunate creature.
CLERK: Orlando?

The CLERK*, an industrious little man in a lawyer's wig, stands at some distance.*

ORLANDO: Yes?
CLERK: You are the one known as Orlando?

ORLANDO: I am. And—you are?

The CLERK *collects himself:*

CLERK: I engage you today by the authority vested in me by the Courts, namely the Chancery Court, the arm of justice under her Majesty, the Queen Victoria.
It is my gravest duty to inform you that you have been made a party to two major lawsuits—preferred against you regarding the matter of your monies, lands and titles.
The chief charges are herein:
One—that you are the Lord Orlando, Earl to Elizabeth, and are long dead—and therefore cannot hold any property whatsoever;
Two—that you are the Lady Orlando, a well known member of Society, and a woman—
which amounts to much the same thing.
How do you plead?

ORLANDO: Plead?
It is not for a Lord to plead, sir—

CLERK: Ah! Then it is Lord Orlando—

ORLANDO: Nor is it for a Lady to be spoken to thus haughtily!

CLERK: I … see …

ORLANDO: All I can say, with any certainty, is that I am Orlando.

CLERK: But to *which* Orlando do I speak
and as such which lawsuit do I deliver?

ORLANDO: I suppose the Lord has not existed for some three hundred years now—

CLERK: Ah! [*Writing*] Lord … Orlando … dead.

ORLANDO: However, the Lady too is gone.
I am sorry to say, but I believe you speak to another Orlando altogether—
and whether this Orlando is more Lord or Lady it is impossible yet to say.

CLERK: You mean to say you exist in a state of utter ambiguity
so that the Court cannot be certain whether you are man or woman, Earl or non-entity,
alive or dead?!

ORLANDO: I should hope I am not dead, sir—

CLERK: I am at quite a loss for how to proceed!

The Lady Orlando requires one set of paperwork—and the deceased quite another.

Without certainty, I cannot deliver *either* suit, and the entire set of proceedings shall be held up in court on account of you residing in a state of *incognito!* Or—*incognita*—as the case may be …

But no matter—we have our own means of making such determinations.

Consulting his paperwork—

Now—how long do you take to dress?

ORLANDO: To dress?

I suppose … No more than ten minutes.

CLERK: And as such can be no self-respecting Lady—

Yet, for a gentleman, you are queerly attired …

How should you respond if, in your presence, I were to kick a spaniel?

ORLANDO: I should gasp, sir! And no doubt weep, for I am excessively tender-hearted.

CLERK: [*moving to write it down*] Excellent—

ORLANDO: But then I should kick you, sir, for your callousness and cruelty.

CLERK: I see …

In what areas are you learned?

ORLANDO: I have read reams and reams of Shakespeare. But I am unversed in geography and find mathematics intolerable.

CLERK: This is *very* clear—

ORLANDO: I am also, myself

a poet.

CLERK: A poet? Of what variety?

ORLANDO: Of the heart, sir.

CLERK: A Romantic. This counts against you whomever you may be—

Finally, are you, in fact, alive or dead?

ORLANDO: …

I'm sorry?

CLERK: Are you deceased, sir.

ORLANDO: I am beginning to wish that I was—

CLERK: [*holding up his hand*] This will do.
In the interests of coming to any conclusion whatsoever—
we determine that—
disregarding your lack of modesty in dress,
your threats of violence to my person and your ambitions to writing poetry of whatever kind—
we pronounce you indisputably, and beyond the shadow of a doubt, Lady Orlando.
… however unorthodox a one.

ORLANDO: I am glad to have assisted you with your paperwork, sir.
May I now be on my way?

CLERK: [*holding up a hand to stop them*] In *light* of this verdict—
the estates which have been held in Chancery until such a time as this matter is resolved are now desequestrated in perpetuity, and descend and are tailed and entailed only in default of marriage.

ORLANDO: I'm sorry?

CLERK: You are required
to take a husband.

ORLANDO: There won't *be* any husband—I can assure you of that!
I'm in pursuit of life and a lover! Not life and a *husband.*

CLERK: If you do not marry
you face destitution.
All your money and possessions should now pass to your husband—
if you have no husband, you shall have no home, no titles, nor even two pennies to rub together.

ORLANDO: What?
But—this is preposterous! I am still Orlando, as I was when the estate was promised to me.
Whether the deed says Lord or Lady does surely not change that fact.

CLERK: Madam—
Your change of self may not have altered your identity
but it has altered your future.
You may well be a Romantic, but in this age
the vagaries of the individual matter little
against the iron countenance
of the Law.

BRIDE: Married when the year is new, he'll be loving, kind and true.

The CLERK *is gone—and a* SUPERSTITIOUS BRIDE *has emerged from the fog, murmuring to herself.*

When February birds do mate, must not wed or dread your fate.
If you wed when March winds blow, joy and sorrow both you'll know.
Marry in April when you can, joy for Maiden and for Man.
Something borrowed, something blue
Something old, something new
And a sixpence in your shoe—
sixpence! I forgot my sixpence!

She stops dead.

Spare, oh spare me, evil fates! Come not out from your horrid den
Curse me not on my wedding day!

ORLANDO: Madam—are you—quite alright?

She turns to ORLANDO *in terror.*

BRIDE: I have forgot my sixpence.

ORLANDO: Oh. Are you—in someone's debt?

BRIDE: It is my wedding day!
It is an ill omen for a bride to forget her sixpence.
[*Lowering her voice*] How else am I to be protected from evil spirits?

ORLANDO: Evil spirits?

BRIDE: Brides are especially vulnerable.
I have taken great care not to let a dog or a nun cross my path today
Nor glance in a mirror after I dressed
Last night I tickled my cat's nose with a feather for hours so that he would sneeze
All this for luck
But all, all is for nothing without a sixpence!

ORLANDO: Madam—surely forgetting such a trinket on one's wedding day cannot be so calamitous?

BRIDE: If my marriage fails and I am left without a husband—
who shall protect me from the robber?
Scare the wild beast?

Anything may lurk in this never-ending fog.
I live in fear of ghosts in the corridors
Monsters under the bed
Every gust of wind through the house may be a spirit calling
Every squeak behind the wainscot the devil's hound—
Terrors are all around us in these dark and uncertain times.
Without a husband, whom shall be my safeguard?

ORLANDO: Madam—please—you must get a hold of yourself!
I know a Lady must feign weakness so as not to offend her male companions
but it seems you have gone rather too far!
We are not in the company of men now—you may admit
you are fit to protect yourself.

BRIDE: But we are the weaker sex, ma'am!
I cannot run in skirts!
I am not even sure of the last time I saw my legs—
my muscles have lost their pliancy from so little use.
I *must* put my faith in the protection of a husband.
But wait!
I have sewed the sixpence into my hem!
Praise the Lord.

She sighs in relief. A black wedding veil is lowered over her face. She processes on and away.

ORLANDO: Heaven help us! Has everyone in this age taken leave of their senses?

REFORMER: Are you lost, my little lamb?

A well-dressed man in a cravat appears, carrying a cane.

ORLANDO: I'm sorry?

REFORMER: It is late for one so fair to be out of doors.
Does not your husband wish you home, my pet?

ORLANDO: I have no husband
Nor home, for that matter.

REFORMER: Is that so?
Poor sweet dear.

He takes a step towards her—

You mean to say
you have nowhere to go
and must now—walk the streets in search of fortune?

ORLANDO: 'Tis a rather bleak assessment, sir
but for the most part, I suppose, 'tis true.

REFORMER: Well then, my sweet little dear. How very—fortuitous that we should meet this night.

ORLANDO: —pardon?

REFORMER: I spend my nights searching the streets for—women of ill-repute. I am well-acquainted with your kind.
But fear not
I am not one of those degenerates who give in to their basest instincts
who soil themselves with pleasure and sin
No—
I am a pillar of the community—
An elected member of the House of Commons
and I am *especially* devoted to the salvation of—wayward women.

ORLANDO: Wayward—

REFORMER: The rehabilitation of such ladies is for me, a veritable obsession—
I think of nothing else.
I have visited with eighty or ninety such creatures in their lodging houses
to—take tea, and
talk
long into the night.
My moral constitution is such that I can tread the path of temptation and emerge, clean of conscience—
It is true, on occasion I am moved to almost lyrical praise of their beauty (inevitably in Italian)—
but should I find I have shown *any* sign of excitation in their presence, I hold myself to the strictest possible discipline, and upon my return home,
subject myself
to the whip.

ORLANDO: Sir! Please!
I fear there has been a—grave misunderstanding. I am in no need of your aid.

REFORMER: It is *redemption* I offer you, my sweetling.
Allow me to—rehabilitate you
for the purpose of marriage.

ORLANDO: Marriage, again! Can this age imagine no other destiny?

REFORMER: What greater fortune is there for a woman consigned to the streets
than to be restored to her proper place in the home?
It is the Gentleman who should venture out into the world
facing all peril and trials
And the Lady who should remain at home, safe and sound.

ORLANDO: This I flatly disbelieve.
You shall not convince me, sir, that a Lady should be destined for such a narrow life.

REFORMER: This is not opinion, my dear, but fact.
Simply ask the naturalist—the taxonomist—the biologist—
men of the new Sciences who look to Nature and see that everything on Earth has a proper place
Mammal and reptile
Bird and amphibian—
Man and woman.
He, with his superior powers of intellect, belongs to law court, office, laboratory—
and she with her—lesser aptitudes to house and home.

ORLANDO: How absurd. And you say this is some fact of nature?
It does not sound at all natural to me—
especially this invention you call Marriage!
Love, I have known
Life and liberty I have enjoyed
But to demand that a woman must live, shut up indoors,
till the end of her days, living only for husband and child? I've never heard anything so unnatural in my life.
And *I* am Orlando, bound for whatever destiny I may choose—
whatever my heart desires.

REFORMER: My dear, I can assure you from my own experience
women do not have desires.
Some may sell their wares to gentlemen callers, but only out of desperation.
And a wife may submit to her husband on occasion, but only to please him. She requires no gratification for herself.

ORLANDO: And I can assure you from *my* own experience
that many a Lady quite enjoy the delights of life
the pursuits of pleasure
and would even declare that nothing could be more delicious.

The REFORMER *stops. His manner switches in an instant.*

REFORMER: Madam
I was under the impression you were some lost soul
forced to these nighttime exploits by necessity—
but you mean to imply that you *enjoy* them?
Then you are one of these New Women
so-called 'modern' creatures who shun the modesty of marriage
and flaunt their wantonness for all to see.

ORLANDO: I thought you were well-acquainted with such wantonness, my Lord—
that you were rather *obsessed* with it—

REFORMER: [*spluttering*] How dare you!
It is not *I* who desire such women, it is *they* who tempt *me*!
My concern—is for the welfare of husband and wife, of the *family*!
The cornerstone of the British Empire, in dire need of our protection
from women who would seduce men away from their loving wives
and toward their basest instincts
drawing civilisation down into disarray and disorder.
And you, unnatural creature, you are one of these would turn our world upside down!

ORLANDO: I hardly see how my remaining unmarried should bring about such catastrophe—

REFORMER: First, it's women refusing to wed
then they're smoking in the street
riding bicycles to and fro
crying out for the vote

And what next?
Men in the home? Women in the House of Lords? Ladies taking jobs—taking *wives*?
Everything shall be turned on its head! It is madness!

ORLANDO: It is not I, sir, that is mad! It is this whole country that seems to have been possessed by weddings and wives! I want no part of it. Can you not simply leave me be? My destiny is no-one's business but my own.

REFORMER: I will tell you what your destiny shall be.
You have lost your house and home
and as such are *destined* for the poorhouse
the jailhouse
or the madhouse.
You may dream on some great destiny, my dear
but a dream is all it shall ever be.
They would fain bury us in their Houses or Beds
as in a Grave

BRIDE: *Women live like Bats or Owls*
Labour like Beasts
And die like Worms.

The REFORMER *is gone, and a* MAD BRIDE *with wild hair stands in his place.*

ORLANDO: Is this … poetry, madam?
It is rather grim
Although it has the ring of truth about it …

She laughs maniacally.

BRIDE: *Alas! a woman that attempts the pen*
Such an intruder on the rights of men.

A wedding bell chimes—her laughter ceases, and she becomes savage.

No!! Not yet—I'm not ready!
I want to run to the top of the tallest hill and feel myself forever and ever and ever alone! I want to venture into the busy world, towns, regions full of life I have heard of but never seen! I'll not submit to sitting indoors, staring at the wallpaper, listening to the clock, tick—tick—tick—

A GENTLEMAN *produces a veil as two others wrestle the screaming* BRIDE *into submission. The veil is drawn over her mouth, face, wild hair—she is concealed from view. Docile as a lamb now, she processes away.*

And far off, thunder rumbles. ORLANDO *shivers.*

ORLANDO: I must not forget all that I am.
I still have my poet's heart!
For—

Remembering—

Nature ...
Doth teach us all to have aspiring minds:
Our souls, whose faculties can comprehend ...
Can comprehend—
But how can I think when my husband is home for tea in an hour
And the scones—he will be wanting them warmed.

Thunder rumbles.

What voice is this?! It is not Orlando's.
Come, Orlando, speak again!

Again, remembering ...

Our souls, whose faculties can comprehend
The wondrous architecture of the world,
And measure every wandering planet's course,
Still climbing after ...
Still climbing ...
... always moving
Until we reach—
And yet—have I left the coals burning in the stove?
I must buy thread, those curtains need mending,
The children will be wanting new shoes—
Children? I am poisoned, *poisoned*!

I need another self.

They call out—

Orlando?
Orlando!

Thunder rumbles and lightning cracks—

ORLANDO, *remembering—*

Lands shall be granted you,
houses assigned you, titles bequeathed upon you
You shall know the glory of high achievement
And nothing you desire shall be denied you.

But I have no desires
And I cannot run in these skirts
Who shall open the carriage door for me
and protect me from the wild beast?
No!!
[*Calling out*] Come, Orlando!
I am sick to death of this self!
I want another!
I need another landscape
another age!

The veiled BRIDES *appear in the fog, amassing around* ORLANDO ...

BRIDES: On all things dark or doubtful let the veil of Purity descend
Virgin I am and ever shall be
/ Not for me the fruitful fields and fertile vineyards
My veil covers my eyes
I do not see
Modesty, modesty!
Speak not, reveal not.

... *and the* GENTLEMEN ...

GENTLEMEN: / Blessed are The Respectable
who prefer to see not,
desire to know not,
who love the darkness
and abhor the light,
which unveils the shameful.
Blessed are those who guard Virtue,
For it has given us Harmony,
Balance
Order—

As they intone, ORLANDO *pulls a dark substance out from their bodice—it is an endless veil, pulled out and out from their stomach ...*

ORLANDO: I am poisoned, through and through!
Is this it, then? Is this my great destiny?
Is the world
in all its variety
shrunk to this?
If I must be a bride
Then I wish to marry Life itself
I wish to be Nature's bride!
To give myself to the embrace of the grass
and the expanse of the sky
I will dream wild dreams
And wax and wane with the moon
Shift and change with the seasons
in Nature, which knows not confinement, only freedom!

A low rumble.

But that is not what the men of Science say.
Everything, it seems, has its place.

Then even Nature has forsaken me.
I have not a single illusion left.
I have sought happiness through many ages and not found it
Fame, and not known it
Love—and missed it
Poetry—and behold, it is meaningless.

Perhaps it is finally time
to make an end
to accept my fate.
As the Old Queen said—
All ends in death ...

ORLANDO *begins to process forward as all the* BRIDES *have before them ...*

—and out of the fog steps a new figure.

SHELMERDINE: Good morrow. Are you lost?

ORLANDO: No. I am dead.

SHELMERDINE: Dear me!
Although I must say
You seem quite lively for a corpse.

ORLANDO: 'Tis my spirit that has died
For I have consigned myself to my fate
And you, no doubt, are here to finish the job!
Go on, then—marry me at your pleasure—
but get it over with, will you, and with haste!

SHELMERDINE: What a peculiar thing, to meet a stranger and at once think of marriage.

ORLANDO *looks at them for the first time.*

ORLANDO: I quite agree.
Then—you are not possessed by an overwhelming desire to be a husband?

SHELMERDINE: Dear God, no. I am far too changeable to commit to being simply 'husband.' I could no more settle on a single self than I could stay in one place. I go where the wind takes me.

ORLANDO: You are an explorer?

SHELMERDINE: Indeed. My life is spent in the most desperate and splendid of adventures.
Every day a new sight, a new exploit.

ORLANDO: How marvellous.

SHELMERDINE: And you—
despite your—passionate words
something tells me that you do not, in fact, harbour a burning wish to become a wife?

ORLANDO: Dear God, no! I can think of nothing worse than being a wife in this age
living the same life, day in, day out, till the end of my days.
How can I, when out there is the world
/ in all its variety.

SHELMERDINE: / in all its variety.

They look at each other.

ORLANDO: Yes.

I feel somehow as if I know you, madam—
Or, sir?

SHELMERDINE: I am Marmaduke Bonthrop Shelmerdine
if one wishes to be formal.
But I prefer
Shel.

ORLANDO: Of course! For there is something romantic and chivalrous about you which rather suits such a wild and dark-plumed name.

SHELMERDINE: I am pleased to hear it.
And you, sir—or madam?

ORLANDO: I am Orlando.

SHELMERDINE: I might have guessed it! For there is something passionate and melancholy about you which is best expressed in the name, 'Orlando.'

ORLANDO: I quite agree.

SHELMERDINE: And how, my dear, did such an remarkable being as yourself come to find themselves here? Demanding to be married?

ORLANDO: I was once Earl to a Queen
Toast of Society
and a poet.
But alas, all are dead.

SHELMERDINE: I am most sorry to hear it.
What was the cause?

ORLANDO: Beaten down by the spirit of this age.
What good is a poet's heart against the iron will of the law
The certainty of Science
The finality of Marriage?
All that is left now is this pale shadow that shall be wife and mother, and nothing more.

SHELMERDINE: This seems rather against your nature.

ORLANDO: Indeed. But it is as the men of Science say—
even in Nature
everything has its proper place
its sphere.

SHELMERDINE: What a peculiar assertion!
My dear Orlando, that may well be what men of Science declare, but it is not at all what Nature says.

ORLANDO: How do you mean?

SHELMERDINE: My adventures have taken me to many territories
in these strange and uncertain times—
including the brave new world of biology.

There is a flower
Pink-petalled and green of stem
But it has jaws that close around any creature that may touch it
and feeds not on sunlight, but flesh and blood.
A strange flower indeed—*Dionaea muscipula*
or more commonly, Venus flytrap.

I have seen a mammal from the other side of the world
which dwells both on land and in water.
It has the bill and webbed feet of a duck
Fur that glows green under certain light
And an ability to lay eggs like a snake.
This creature they call *Platypus anatinus.*

And here—

SHELMERDINE *produces, bright against the dark fog, a flower.*

This, my friend, is the four-winged saltbush
It grows in a great bright mass across western parts of the Americas.
Nothing could be more common—
and nothing more extraordinary
for what is most fascinating
is that in summer, it grows male buds
but come winter
only female flowers.

ORLANDO: But—how can that be?

SHELMERDINE: My dear Orlando, Nature *delights* in mystery!
It plays queer tricks on us all
most especially the naturalists, taxonomists and biologists—
any who attempt to pin it down.
Whatever category they may construct—
there is something in Nature that will overflow it.

ORLANDO: How extraordinary.
If only one could say the same of humankind.

SHELMERDINE: This is best of all, my friend:
it appears, should one look to Science
that even the most typical of the human species are as genetically diverse
as snowflakes.
The truth is,
nothing is any longer one thing.
Why, therefore, should you be?
ORLANDO: How invigorating
to see the world again, in all its variety.
But whatever Nature may tell us
There is still this age to contend with
and whatever small destiny it has in mind for us.
SHELMERDINE: Perhaps.
But then again, in an age where so much is uncertain
so much is being discovered—being created—
perhaps anything is possible.
Take this question of marriage, for instance.
I have made friends, in my travels, with a Ms Toklas and Ms Stein
respectable women both,
and these ladies live together, write together—
and also share a bed.
Then there's my friend Mrs Ellis,
who revels in the love of men and women—
and so does her husband.
They are quite content together.
And of course, there are my dear friends Fanny and Stella,
Who met at Eton College as boys
but now live together as wives.
Many a pair that have forged their own way.
ORLANDO: How marvellous.
Do you think, then, that it could be marriage
if one's wife insists each day on venturing into the town square by herself?
If she spends her nights not tending to the dishes
but writing poetry?

SHELMERDINE: Could it be marriage
if one's husband is always off exploring new territories,
and sailing around the Cape?

ORLANDO: Could it be marriage if one doesn't wish to have children?
Or occasionally falls in love with other people?

SHELMERDINE: Could it be marriage
if you were one day man and wife
the next day, wife and man
and some days both and neither?

ORLANDO: Oh Shel—could marriage be such a thing, perhaps I would rather like it.

SHELMERDINE: Much more is possible than what is sanctioned
if one is brave enough to think it.
Look at the curious inventions of our new world!
There is a device by which I may now speak to someone in Belgium or Belize, all without leaving London!
Perhaps one day I shall be able to travel there through the air—
fly to Italy for afternoon tea and the moon itself for supper.

ORLANDO: Perhaps, in the future, one may drive through the streets in a carriage that moves of its own accord—
one may come home after dark, and at a touch, a whole room shall be lit.

SHELMERDINE: A building might be hundreds of stories high, and one may shoot through the air from one floor to another.

ORLANDO: There might be an eyeglass that allows one to see the world so closely, that every particle of which we are made will become clear
the matter that makes up our flesh, the sky, the stars …

SHELMERDINE: Perhaps, in the future, women may wear breeches, and men skirts—

ORLANDO: Lords tend the home and ladies take public office—
Or no such distinctions will be made any longer,
and each will choose their destiny according to their nature …

Thunder rumbles.

ORLANDO: And until then?

SHELMERDINE: We find our way through.

ORLANDO: I think I am beginning to understand …

All this to say
Marmaduke Bonthrop Shelmerdine

Will you marry me?
SHELMERDINE: Of course, my dear Orlando.
And then I must be off
There is much more of this world left to explore.
And you,
dear Orlando,
will you marry me?
ORLANDO: Of course, darling Shel.
But then I must be on my way
I feel the whole world opening itself up to me.
And some new self, perhaps, beginning to emerge …
SHELMERDINE: Then it's settled.

SHELMERDINE *offers their hand.* ORLANDO *shakes it.*

ORLANDO: Until we meet again—my Shel.
SHELMERDINE: Best of luck to you,
Orlando.

SHELMERDINE *kisses* ORLANDO*'s hand, and melts away.*

ORLANDO *stands for a moment, then follows them.*

Thunder rumbles, and lightning flashes—until—

ACT FOUR

—and the lightning becomes the flickering lights of a passing tube—

And a fourth ORLANDO *sits on a tube platform in a puffer jacket and Docs. They're surrounded by a throng of modern citizens, each in their own inner world.* ORLANDO *takes it all in.*

A YOUTH *seated next to* ORLANDO*—*

YOUTH: Excuse me—have you got the time?
ORLANDO: I'm sorry?

YOUTH *indicates wrist.*

[*Finds they have a watch*] Oh—it's—twenty minutes past ten.
YOUTH: Cheers.
ORLANDO: Could you tell me
where exactly we are?
YOUTH: St Paul's, mate.
ORLANDO: St Paul's … This is London?
YOUTH: [*with a strange look*] Yeah …
ORLANDO: It doesn't look like St Paul's.
YOUTH: Well … we're underground.
ORLANDO: Underground?
YOUTH: This is the Tube? Runs all the way underneath the city? You feeling alright, mate?
ORLANDO: A whole world beneath our feet …

The tube goes past—lights flicker out—flicker back—

—revealing ORLANDO*, same position, and a* BUSINESSWOMAN*, phone in one hand, roller bag in the other—*

BUSINESSWOMAN: My flight's not till one p.m. Eight hours in the air but I'll be in New York for dinner if you care to join. Back tomorrow night. Ooh! Can we go to that Chinese place on Long Island? The noodles here are rubbish.
How a people can invade most of Asia and Africa and not ever learn how to season food properly is beyond me.

Another tube—lights flicker out—

*And back on—*ORLANDO, *and three* BARRISTERS, *with smart white shirts, black robes and briefcases, wearing or holding white wigs—*

ONE: We're definitely going to be delayed—

TWO: Bollocks.

ONE: I'd say ten minutes at least.

TWO: Every time it snows this whole system goes to shit. You'd think the whole city was frozen over.

ONE: All the power of modern science, the combustion engine, complex computing, and we're completely undone by a little bit of weather.

THREE: I thought it didn't snow in London anymore. Urban heat or something. From the buildings.

TWO: Well, it bloody started up again when I decided to move here. Now there's always a risk of surprise snow.

ONE: More like fifteen minutes, I reckon.

TWO: Bollocks!!

Lights out—lights back—

ORLANDO *and a* WOMAN *surrounded by shopping bags, typing into her phone and muttering aloud—*

WOMAN: Bath salts—soy candle—linen sheets for the double bed—

Lights out—

Lights back—a LESBIAN COUPLE *holding hands—*

ONE: I hope they're doing a roast. I bloody love a roast.
Which wine did you get?

TWO: A nice chardonnay from Shropshire.

ONE: Shropshire? These aren't our artist friends, these are *home-owners*. You couldn't have picked up something a little more sophisticated?

TWO: There are perfectly good vineyards in middle England now, the climate's gotten just as warm as it is in the South of France. It's actually getting *too* hot in Burgundy or Champagne or wherever. Give it a few years, the French'll be out, and everyone'll be clamouring for a drop from Shropshire.

Lights flicker out—

*Lights back—*ORLANDO *and three very stoned* YOUNG PEOPLE*—*

ONE: Woaaahhh
that tube was goin
so slowww

TWO: Hahahaha

THREE: What you talkin bout, bruv
My head is spinning man
it was going super fast
like
speed of light fast

TWO: The thing is, you're both right
Coz time is relative, bruv

ONE: Bruv!

THREE: Bruv.

TWO: It's all relative
We're all having our own subjective experiences of the world, bruv, you get me?
So like how do you know what's even real?
That's the thing
You don't

ONE: Do you ever actually *think* about the speed of light?

THREE: Uh, no? I actually don't?

ONE: Nah, listen, listen!
Do you ever think about the speed of light and how actually
when you look into the night sky
into space
you're looking
back in time.

THREE: Bruv.

TWO: Bruv!

Lights out—lights back—

ORLANDO *and a* POLICE OFFICER.

ORLANDO: Excuse me
Could you tell me where exactly everyone's going?

OFFICER: This is the Circle Line.

ORLANDO: And where does that lead to?

OFFICER: It doesn't *lead* anywhere. It's a Circle. Goes round and round Central London.
Where do you want to go?

ORLANDO: I—I don't know.

OFFICER: What do you mean, you don't know?
You have to know where you're going.

Lights out—lights back—two TEENAGERS—

ONE: Nothing you desire will be denied you—
you just have to get in touch with your inner power.
I'm serious!
You can have whatever you want, you just have to know exactly what it is, and be able to hold it in mind, really clearly.

TWO: I just think maybe I've set the bar too high to manifest an estate with land and three hundred and sixty-five rooms when I still can't really afford my rent, you know?

ONE: Maybe you need a vision board.

Lights out—lights back—two GYM-GOERS—

GYM-GOER 1: Keep your eye on the target. Meditation, affirmations, cold plunges. It's all about balance. The Greeks knew it. Order. Discipline. Inwards and outwards.

GYM-GOER 2: Train the body, train the mind, right?

GYM-GOER 1: That's why we're high-value individuals—destined for greatness.

GYM-GOER 2: Look out, world—we're going places.

Lights out—lights back. Three HIGH-SCHOOL STUDENTS *with ties and crisp uniforms.*

SCHOOLKID 1: A-levels—early acceptance into Oxford—first-class honours—summer internships—Bar—Junior partner—senior partner—retire early. Twenty years.

SCHOOLKID 2: County—District—Regional champ—Nationals—Relay team for a bit—Worlds—Olympic qualifications—podium—then move into sports media—maybe a little panel show. Twelve years.

SCHOOLBOY: Engaged within two to a handsome doctor—down payment—nice garden—kid one—kid two—second home in a nice school catchment—rent out the first—Labrador. Ten years.

*Lights out—lights back—*ORLANDO, *and an elegant-looking older* WOMAN *with several suitcases. She taps* ORLANDO *on the shoulder.*

WOMAN: Excuse me, sir. Oh sorry—Miss? Sorry, which is it?
ORLANDO: Uh—both. Neither.
WOMAN: Oh. Wonderful. Could you help me with my bags? I'm getting on the next one, if you don't mind helping me on.
What about you? Where are you headed?

Lights out—lights back—

Two STUDENTS—

STUDENT 1: Have you ever wondered
if you've like said a sentence
and been the first person in all of history
to say those exact words
in that exact order?
STUDENT 2: Huh.
STUDENT 1: Emerald—pineapple—olive tree.
STUDENT 2: Emerald pineapple olive tree.

Lights out—lights back—two service WORKERS, *in uniform.*

WORKER 1: Get a degree they said
WORKER 2: Right
WORKER 1: Work hard they said
WORKER 2: Right
WORKER 1: Stay on the path
WORKER 2: Right
WORKER 1: You'll have a bright future
WORKER 2: Right
WORKER 1: Now I have three degrees, I'm living in a sharehouse and serving prosecco to Australian kids on their gap year.
And I'm like, shit—is this really my destiny?

*Lights out—lights back—*ORLANDO *on a platform full of people lost in their phones, and a bespectacled* PROFESSOR *in an ill-fitting suit, talking to a young* REPORTER *recording the conversation on their phone—*

PROFESSOR: This is an age marked by the excessive, the indulgent and the self-involved. There's no respect for the old orders, just an obsession with the new. If my students can't find the word that 'feels' right to them, they simply make one up! The passions have always been an unruly guide. That way lies chaos …

ORLANDO *notices a person in snow gear who looks suspiciously like a modern* SASHA, *in fur coat and boots. They look at* ORLANDO *and smile.*

Lights out—

Lights back—a TOUR GUIDE *and a gaggle of* AUSTRALIAN TOURISTS *with backpacks and Blundstones—*

TOUR GUIDE: Next we'll be heading to Aldgate Station.
Now some of the brickwork you'll see contains parts of an old Roman Wall. The site has seen Viking and Saxon and Norman invasions, and survived the Great Fire of London. It's been a graveyard for plague victims, a bomb shelter during the Blitz, a station for steam and now electric trains, and even a wartime archive for the National Gallery and British Museum, from the Elgin Marbles to the famous portrait of Queen Elizabeth herself.
It's a place that has lived many lives, you might say. It's no longer one thing.
At every point in history this City has survived through constant reinvention. Becoming itself anew.

Light out—lights back—

Three PROTESTORS *with Extinction Rebellion gear. One is tapping furiously on their phone. A* BUSKER *sits on the other end of the platform. They have a guitar slung over their shoulder and a jester's hat full of loose change next to them.*

PROTESTER 1: How do you spell 'kleptomaniacal'?
PROTESTER 2: Why?
PROTESTER 1: I'm writing Yelp reviews for the British Museum.
PROTESTER 3: Long live the Revolution.

ORLANDO *looks at the* BUSKER *with the jester's hat—they look back—*

Lights out—lights back—

ORLANDO, *and a* SCIENTIST *excitedly talking to their* PARTNER—

SCIENTIST: Just as Euclid's theories gave way to Newton's, and Newton's to Einstein's—there are no certainties any more—everything is relative to everything else—which means there are no basic principles—nothing is any longer one thing. And *that* begs the question—where is it all going? Where does it all end? The only logical answer is it *doesn't*—this process of questioning, of revisioning, will just go on and on and on—

Lights out—lights back—a group of PARTYGOERS *dressed up as if for Heaven nightclub—totally transformed from their everyday selves—dancing, singing—*

*Lights out—lights back—*ORLANDO*, alone, on the platform.*

ORLANDO: Perhaps I am beginning to understand …

Orlando?
Orlando!

Lights out—lights back—

And seven different modern ORLANDO*s occupy the tube—*ORLANDO*s we recognise, and new* ORLANDO*s—one with a book, another looking down the platform …*

Lights out—lights back—

Our modern ORLANDO *stands alone again.*

They sit back—make themselves comfortable—and smile.

The tube rattles on.

The lights go out.

THE END

Based in an old factory on Gadigal land, Sydney, Belvoir is one of Australia's most celebrated and beloved theatre companies. Since 1984, when a group of 600 theatre-lovers came together to buy a theatre and save it from becoming an apartment block, Belvoir has been at the forefront of Australian storytelling for the stage.

Each year the company presents an annual season of shows for this now-iconic corner stage. New work and new stories sit at the centre of Belvoir's programming, alongside a mix of reinvented classics and international writing, and a foundational commitment to Indigenous stories. In short, Belvoir is about theatrical invention, an open society, and faith in humanity.

Under the leadership of Artistic Director Eamon Flack and Executive Director Aaron Beach, Belvoir engages Australia's most prominent and promising theatre-makers. Belvoir has nurtured the talents of artists including Cate Blanchett, Simon Stone, Leah Purcell, Benedict Andrews, Tommy Murphy, Kate Mulvany, Anne-Louise Sarks, Wesley Enoch, S. Shakthidharan, and former Artistic Director Neil Armfield. Landmark productions include *Counting and Cracking*, *The Wild Duck*, *FANGIRLS*, *Cloudstreet*, *Barbara and the Camp Dogs*, *The Drover's Wife*, *Jungle and the Sea*, *Angels in America*, *Keating!*, *The Sapphires*, and many, many more. Belvoir regularly tours nationally and internationally.

Belvoir receives government support for its activities from the Federal Government through Creative Australia and the state government through Create NSW.

BELVOIR.COM.AU

BELVOIR EDUCATION

Our Education Program provides students and teachers with insights into the work of Belvoir and first-hand experiences of the theatre-making process.

PERFORMANCES

Inspiring stories, new voices, and great theatre – in the heart of Surry Hills.

Dedicated performances for schools are held throughout the year at Belvoir St Theatre.

NO BARRIERS ACCESS PROGRAM

No Barriers to your students experiencing theatre.

Belvoir's No Barriers Access Program works to remove obstacles to young people experiencing and enjoying theatre. Our programs bring students to Belvoir to see our plays and take workshops to eligible schools.

WORKSHOPS

Belvoir artists work with your students – anywhere, anytime.

Our workshops are run at Belvoir St Theatre, your school (in NSW), or online, at a time of your choosing. Students learn directly from industry artists in practical workshops, exploring performance, design, playwriting, devising, directing, technical production and more!

YOUNG BELVOIR THEATRE CLUB

Theatre makers and audiences of the future.

Our annual theatre club is for young people in Years 10, 11 and 12 who love theatre. Members attend Belvoir productions, gain insight into how productions come together and meet actors and artists.

RESOURCES

Discover how theatre is created.

Go behind the scenes into the world of Belvoir using our collection of resources online. You'll discover virtual tours, design plans and model boxes, promotion style guides, digital programs, interviews, archives and more.

FIRST CLASS

Early teaching career season ticket program.

Gain a deeper understanding of Belvoir's work and processes, connect with colleagues, develop insider industry knowledge, and get direct support and inspiration for your classroom teaching.

EDUCATION ENEWS

Sign up to stay in the loop.

Find out more about upcoming education events, schools performances, workshops and opportunities for teachers and students.

BELVOIR.COM.AU/EDUCATION/

PRODUCTION SUPPORTERS

THE GROUP

SUPPORTING WOMEN-LED CREATIVITY

Thank you to all members of The Group for generously supporting *Orlando* in Belvoir's 2025 season.

Each year a collective of inspiring like-minded women (aka The Group) commit to supporting women creatives and bringing more women's stories to the Belvoir stage. From playwrights to directors, actors, designers, sound technicians, producers and more, The Group support creative leadership and invest in empowering women-led mainstage productions. Members enjoy a range of active networking opportunities and behind the-scenes events.

We invite you to become a member of The Group and join us on the creative journey, 'from page to stage', and to engage with us during the creative development of a women-led work from to rehearsal, all the way up to the opening night.

BELVOIR SUPPORTERS

PATRONS

Her Excellency the Honourable Margaret Beazley AC KC Governor of New South Wales.

TRUSTS AND FOUNDATIONS

John & Libby Fairfax

Mountain Air Foundation

BELVOIR GIVING CIRCLES

ARTISTIC DIRECTOR'S CIRCLE

Led by Belvoir Artistic Director Eamon Flack, the Artistic Director's Circle supports an iconic Belvoir show each year; recent supported productions include *Into the Woods* in 2023, *August: Osage County* in 2024 and *King Lear* in 2025. Being a member of the Artistic Director's Circle is a rewarding opportunity to take an active role in Belvoir's development and contribute to our most ambitious work.

Patty Akopiantz & Justin Punch
Sophie & Stephen Allen
The Balnaves Foundation
Guido Belgiorno-Nettis AM & Michelle Belgiorno-Nettis
Anne Britton
Jillian Broadbent AC FRSN
Andrew Cameron AM & Cathy Cameron
Sue Donnelly
David Gonski AC & Orli Wargon OAM
Fee & David Hancock
Ingrid Kaiser
Alison Kitchen
Ian Learmonth & Julia Pincus
Helen Lynch AM & Helen Bauer
Sam Meers AO
Karen Moses OAM
Mountain Air Foundation
Beau Neilson
Kerr Neilson
Paris Neilson
Stuart & Kate O'Brien
Cathie & Paul Oppenheim
Dan & Jackie Phillips
Andrew Price
Sherry-Hogan Foundation
Rob Thomas AO
Judy Thomson
The WeirAnderson Foundation
Kim Williams AM & Catherine Dovey
Rosie Williams & John Grill AO

THE GROUP

Patty Akopiantz
Sophie Allen
Jessica Block
Margaret Butler
Louise Campbell
Suzanne Daniel
Johanna Featherstone
Jennie Gao
Jane-Maree Hurley
Kirsty Kovacs
Robin Low
Sandra McCullagh
Sam Meers AO
Karen Moses OAM
Julie-Anne Lacko
Naomi O'Brien
Elizabeth Pakchung
Rebel Penfold-Russell OAM
Sabrina Quick
Sue Rosen
Victoria Tayor
Louise Thurgood-Phillips
Chris Yates
Cathy Yuncken

THE HIVE

THE HIVE is a community of professionals and creatives, connected through a love of theatre. Donations to THE HIVE support a new work at Belvoir each year, starting with *The Wrong Gods* in 2025, to help pave the way for the next generation of theatre-makers in Sydney and beyond.

HIVE AMBASSADORS

Dan Chesterman
Johanna Featherstone
Piers Grove
Alicia Gunn
Zach Kitschke
Tommy Murphy
Teya Phillips
Matt Rossi

HIVE MEMBERS

Brian Abel
Mollie Anderson
Alex Badran
Aaron Beach
Justin Butterworth
Jake Blundell
Michael Cameron
James M Garvey
Rosemary Hannah & Lynette Preston
Samantha Jones
Clancy King
Nicolas Mason
Catriona Morgan-Hunn
Nathan Moses
Julia Newbould
Salleigh Olsen
Leigh Sanderson
Steph Sands
Dain Thomas
Martyn Thompson

BELVOIR DONORS

Thank you to the visionary donors who have committed to a level of financial support that allows us to realise our creative ambitions and share passionate, diverse and surprising contemporary Australian theatre with audiences here, across the country and across the globe.

$50,000 AND ABOVE

The Balnaves Foundation
Blake Beckett Trust
Andrew Cameron AM & Cathy Cameron
Doc Ross Family Foundation
John & Libby Fairfax
The Kerridge Foundation
Anne & Mark Lazberger
Ian Learmonth & Julia Pincus
Karen Moses OAM
The Neilson Foundation
The Nelson Meers Foundation
Oranges & Sardines Foundation

$20,000-$49,999

Stephen & Sophie Allen
Copyright Agency Cultural Fund
Gandevia Foundation
Girgensohn Foundation
Hansen Little Foundation
Highgate Foundation
Marion Heathcote & Brian Burfitt
Victoria Holthouse
Anita Jacoby AM
Ingrid Kaiser
The Keir Foundation
James N Kirby Foundation
The Knights Family Jabula Foundation
Ross Littlewood & Alexandra Curtin
Helen Lynch AM & Helen Bauer
Millari Family Trust
Mountain Air Foundation
Cathie & Paul Oppenheim

$10,000-$19,999

Patty Akopiantz & Justin Punch
Guido Belgiorno-Nettis AM & Michelle Belgiorno-Nettis
Anne Britton
Jillian Broadbent AC FRSN
Jan Burnswoods
Daughters of Penelope
Bob & Chris Ernst
Louise Flanagan
Johnson Family Foundation
Libby Higgin & Dr Gae Anderson
Tan Kueh & Family
Matana Foundation
Cynthia Nadai & Roslyn Burge
Panthera
Plenary Group
David Pumphrey OAM & Jill Pumphrey
The Roberts Pike Foundation
Patagorang Foundation
Matthew Rossi
Penelope Seidler AM
Victoria Taylor
Judy Thomson
The Wales Family Foundation
The WeirAnderson Foundation
Shemara Wikramanayake & Ed Gilmartin
Rosie Williams & John Grill AO
Kim Williams AM & Catherine Dovey
Toni Wren

$5,000-$9,999

Colin & Richard Adams
Elizabeth Allen & David Langley
Jessica Block
Dan & Emma Chesterman
Chrysanthemum Foundation
Holly Coleman
Bernard Coles KC & Margaret Coles
Constructability Recruitment
Hartley & Sharon Cook
Sue Donnelly
Rachel Emma Ferguson Foundation
Freilich Prescribed Private Fund
Mark & Jane Fulton
Danny & Kathleen Gilbert
The Greatorex Fund
Jane-Maree Hurley
Zach Kitschke
Robin Love
Julianne Maxwell
Bruce Meagher & Greg Waters
Stuart and Kate O'Brien
Rebel Penfold-Russell OAM
Sue Rosen
Rossi Family Trust
Peter & Jan Shuttleworth
Jessica Singer
Jann Skinner
The Skrzynski Foundation
Juliet and David Walker
Chris & Bea Sochan
Annie Williams
Chris Yates
Cathy Yuncken

SPECIAL THANKS

We thank our Life Members, who have made outstanding contributions to Belvoir over more than thirty years. They have changed the course of the company and are now ingrained in its fabric.

Neil Armfield AO, Neil Balnaves AO, Andrew Cameron AM, David Gonski AC, Rachel Healy, Louise Herron AM, Sue Hill, Geoffrey Rush AC, Orli Wargon OAM, and Chris Westwood.

We would also like to acknowledge our Legacy Donors, for making a dramatic difference by remembering Belvoir in their Wills: Len Armfield, Liz Barton, Brian Carey, Sharan Daly, Nick Enright.

Ronald Falk, Diane Hague, Samantha Jones, Jann Kohlman, Patricia McEnerny, Cajetan Mula, Geoffrey Scharer, Ronald Thompson, and Shirley June Warland. We will always remember their generosity.

Thank you to the generous individuals and Foundations supported the redevelopment of Belvoir Street Theatre and the purchase of our Warehouse in 2005 & 2006, and the renovation of our theatre foyer and bathrooms in 2024.

Andrew & Cathy Cameron
(Refurbishment of theatre and warehouse)

Russell Crowe
(Redevelopment of theatre)

The Gonski Foundation & The Nelson Meers Foundation
(Gonski Meers Foyer)

Andrew & Wendy Hamlin
(Executive Director's office)

Hal Herron
(The Hal Bar)

Nelson Meers Foundation
(Sam's Bar)

Geoffrey Rush
(Redevelopment of theatre)

Fred Street AM
(Upstairs dressing room)

BELVOIR PARTNERS

PATRON

The Honourable Margaret Beazley AC KC,
Governor of New South Wales

GOVERNMENT PARTNERS

MAJOR PARTNERS

ASSOCIATE PARTNERS

SUPPORTING PARTNERS

POOR TOMS

PORTEÑO

MEDIA PARTNERS

If your business would like to partner with Belvoir, please email us at **development@belvoir.com.au** or call **02 8396 6250**